For Maure

At-Home MOTHERHOOD

Making It Work for You

Cindy Tolliver

Cindy Tolliver

Resource Publications, Inc.
San Jose, California

Editorial director: Kenneth Guentert
Managing editor: Elizabeth J. Asborno

Front cover photograph taken by Perry Chow

Reprint Department
Resource Publications, Inc.
160 E. Virginia Street #290
San Jose, California 95112-5876

Library of Congress Cataloging in Publication Data
Tolliver, Cindy, 1951-
    At-home motherhood : making it work for you / Cindy
Tolliver.
        p.   cm.
    Includes bibliographical references and index.
    ISBN 0-89390-295-0
    1. Mothers—United States. 2. Motherhood—United States.
3. Home economics—United States. 4. Self-actualization
(Psychology). I. Title.
HQ759.T67 1994
306.874'3—dc20   93-51506

Printed in the United States of America

98 97 96 95 94 | 5 4 3 2

For Mark, Maggie, Anne and Elizabeth

Contents

Part One: Relationships

Part Two: Business Matters

Part Three: On Your Own

Preface

I've been an at-home mother on and off for sixteen years. The first time was from 1978 to 1982, following the birth of my two oldest daughters. A starry-eyed twenty-something, I loved being the mistress of a house with two babies all my own. Oblivious to all the women out there building careers, I just wanted to build my own nest. Plans for "What if?" contingencies? What for? My future was rock solid.

The blissful baby boom was brief. On its heels followed a series of unexpected character-builders including a divorce and a harrowing period of updating my skills and expertise. I eventually landed a good job, bought a house and set up housekeeping as a single working mom.

Five years later, I married Mark and made a comeback as an at-home mother. We were happily settled in Saratoga, a suburban town near San Jose, California, when little Elizabeth was born. Besides being the picture of health with a sunny disposition, she was also that rarest of species: a baby who's a good sleeper. Everything was perfect. As a mature, fairly experienced mother, I anticipated smooth sailing.

But things weren't as wonderful as I had expected. I was doing exactly what I wanted to, and yet, as soon as everybody headed out the door, my emotions frequently took a nosedive. Frustrated, lonely, and blue, life seemed to be passing me by. I keenly missed the camaraderie and easy laughter and excitement of the high school where I had taught. I didn't think I could tell my husband: I was afraid he would think I was crazy. Worst of all, I had always hated whiners and complainers, but here I was in danger of becoming one.

After several months of private discontent, I'd had enough. I decided to start a self-improvement program to develop a more positive attitude and to leave behind the cloud of negativism that enveloped me. I wanted to enjoy these good years to the fullest.

I began by exploring why my feelings this second time at home were so different from the first. First of all, I realized my attitudes and expectations had changed. This time I brought home the notion that to be truly successful, you had to "do it all." I kept comparing myself unfavorably with all those "successful" women out there in Silicon Valley who were product managers, computer engineers—whatever—jetting around *and* having small children at home. I felt my confidence slipping away. Secondly, having lived through one marriage break-up, I was super-sensitized to my vulnerability as a homemaker. I felt nervous not earning my own money.

Having always considered myself at least average, even "tough," I speculated that others like me were also feeling my worries and discontent and wondering what to do about them. I began to talk to other women about these issues. I read everything I could get my hands on about women who stayed at home. I began to keep a journal of my thoughts as a kind of writing therapy.

My research led me to develop, in collaboration with Lois Kalafus, the theory of the Home Alone Syndrome. I came to believe that being at home alone without adult interaction is inherently depressing. Women must prepare themselves for this and plan how to counteract it. Betty Friedan noticed the

Home Alone Syndrome thirty years ago, but she called it "the problem that has no name." Her solution? Get out of the house and get a job. Fine, but what about the women who wanted to make staying at home a positive and productive experience?

I decided that waiting until "This too shall pass" wasted what could be the happiest, most productive years of a woman's life. It shouldn't have to be that way. And so I hatched the idea of writing a support book for at-home mothers.

I began looking for behavior and attitude patterns that led to happiness on the homefront. My main resource was women who were at home with their kids. I asked them endless questions: What is your support system? What do you do to combat the blues? How do you keep your sanity? Are you happy as a homemaker? Why or why not? Their answers to my questions, my reading, and my personal experience form the basis for the ideas and tips presented in this book.

Will Rogers once said: Even if you're on the right track, you'll get run over if you just sit there. *At-Home Motherhood: Making It Work for You* is a practical, thought-provoking and fun way for the at-home mother to find her "right track" so that she can move and grow in the direction she chooses.

Acknowledgments

I wish to acknowledge the contributions that others have made to the contents of this book. Thanks to Karen Garappolo, whose insight, enthusiasm and accessibility never flagged from start to finish. Also to Phyllis McCormick, Marlaine Griffin, Ellen Sommer, Helen MacKinlay, Pam Cagle, Beth White, Priscilla Ho, Corliss Green, Maureen Risbry and Lydia Fransese for their ideas and encouragement. A special thanks goes to Lois Kalafus, who collaborated with me in the initial stages. And my immense gratitude goes to my colleagues Henci Goer and Alexis Rubin, who brought their intelligence and friendship and sharpened pencils to my kitchen table. Without their valuable editorial assistance, this book would not have been possible. Thank you to the many at-home mothers who generously shared their experiences and their knowledge. I am especially indebted to Helen Tolliver and my own mother, Jean Cagle, for the example they set. I am also grateful to my publisher, Bill and Susan Burns, for giving an unpublished writer a chance, to Ken Guentert for believing in the idea behind this book, and to Liz Asborno, for her careful attention to the manuscript. Finally, thanks to my husband, Mark, for his calm support and to Maggie, Anne and Elizabeth, who tolerated the long hours I spent preoccupied with this book.

Part One

Relationships

1

At Home in Today's Society

She wants to have it all, but not all at once.
— Caroline H., on the "sequencing" woman

Whenmy close friend Ellen asked her mother, now an anthropology professor at the University of California, if her self-identity had suffered during the seventeen years she stayed home raising four daughters, Anne Parker smiled wryly and shot back: "I didn't know I had a separate identity."

Anne's retort illustrates the dizzying changes that have occurred since our mothers' time. Women in the 1950s, like Ellen's mom, had only one socially acceptable choice: be a housewife. In sharp contrast, most of today's at-home mothers truly choose to stay home to raise their children themselves. But this often means giving up a professional identity and all the good things that went with it that form an important part of today's woman's self-image. As a result, she wants, needs and expects different things from staying home than her own mother did and she faces a whole set of issues her own mother never dreamed of.

According to Arlene Rossen Cardozo in her bestseller, *Sequencing*, today's mother often has had a full-time career and

3

is planning on full-time child-rearing as a "sequencing" step. This means that full-time childrearing will be the second segment in a career-home-career plan of "having it all, but not all at once."

At-home motherhood—whether for a season or for a lifetime—is still the top choice of a strong, if silent, majority. According to the 1991 Bureau of Labor statistics, less than thirty-eight percent of married mothers of children under six worked full-time outside the home. Like Mark Twain's death, reports of the at-home mother's demise have been greatly exaggerated.

However, this lifestyle does not come cheap. At-home mothers pay a high price—both economically and emotionally—in order to stay home to care for their children. They are often surprised to find that full-time mothering turns out to be, like the Army recruiting slogan, "the toughest job you'll ever love." Why so tough? First of all, anyone who is home alone—"alone" meaning without other adults to interact with—for a prolonged period, is prone to depression. Women often grossly underestimate the emotional adjustments they need to make in order to cope with the isolation, lack of structure and loss of identity that are part of the job. And if they buy in to the new societal norm that success means "doing it all" at once, they may devalue themselves and the choice they have made. One mother I interviewed referred to herself as a "dinosaur"; another said she felt "like a butterfly turning into a caterpillar." Unfortunately and unfairly, being "just a housewife" just doesn't seem to be enough in today's career-oriented society.

This is where *At-Home Motherhood: Making It Work for You* comes in. Feelings of loneliness, the blues, restlessness, and self-doubt are both predictable and normal when women make the transition from a full-time career to full-time mothering—so much so that I refer to this group of emotional experiences as the Home Alone Syndrome, a term coined by social worker Lois Kalafus. Fortunately, we can prepare for these emotional adjustments and can develop strategies to modify the conditions that promote symptoms of the Home

Alone Syndrome. In this way at-home mothers can move with relative ease past the transition period and settle into the rhythms of a new lifestyle.

Mission and Movement

I got most of the suggestions in this book by searching out and interviewing those individuals who were obviously happy, comfortable and fulfilled in their roles. Posing the all-important question, "What's your secret for finding satisfaction and fulfillment at home full-time?" yielded some interesting answers. Two key concepts contributing to happiness on the homefront cropped up with striking regularity in my interviews:

1. clearly defined goals and sense of purpose—in other words, a sense of mission

2. a capacity for movement, both externally (physical activity) and internally (emotional, spiritual, and intellectual growth).

What Is "Mission?"

The happiest at-home mothers bring home with them a strong sense of purpose and clearly defined goals: They know why they're at home and what they want to accomplish there. By "happy homemakers" I don't mean those perky stereotypes seen in detergent commercials who are contented as cows with laundry that is a brighter bright. I'm referring to women who possess a certain inner quality of happiness derived from quiet confidence and inner calm. Many spoke of the steadying effect of having a mission on which to focus; others spoke of having long-term goals, purposes or projects. The term "mission" seems the most precise for our purposes.

The mission concept is particularly apt because of its association with a "higher calling." A higher calling, often an undertaking inspired by noble reasons (i.e., not for material gain), is right on target for at-home motherhood. Women who have sacrificed a much-needed second paycheck to follow their hearts home would concur. And what could be more noble than bringing up the next generation?

Psychologist/business writer Charles Garfield gives the following working definition of mission: "an image of a desired state of affairs that inspires action, determines behavior, and fuels motivation" (77). People in the business world use written mission statements with great success to help them focus and prioritize. Why not apply this same successful concept to the at-home mother's private enterprise? In this book, then, the word "mission" has almost the same meaning as "goals and purposes." I will guide you in how to formulate and make written statements of your missions, or as Garfield puts it, your "desired state of affairs," for your various roles as an at-home mother.

Women's Movements

A capacity for moving forward is the second factor that contributes to joy on the homefront. Movement implies physical action—exercising, playing with our children, attending meetings, going to class. But movement is also the inner work that propels us on a journey of the mind, the heart or the spirit. Learning, loving, growing, observing, appreciating, listening, understanding—activities that happen in our heads and hearts—are critical to our survival on the homefront. In fact, the inner challenges are the toughest part of the job! Being right in the thick of the action, all the while sitting stock-still in our favorite easy chair, is not a contradiction in terms. As one woman said, "Some of my best ideas and insights come to me while I'm nursing my baby." Defining our mission is only half the equation; the other half is developing both internal and external attitudes and habits that promote the fulfillment of that mission.

Free Choice Makes the Difference

I reared my two sons in the late fifties and early sixties, when my role was clearly differentiated from that of my husband. We had an unspoken agreement that I cooked, cleaned house, tended the garden, did the marketing and took care of the children while he worked at a demanding job and did maintenance on the house and car as well as heavy work in the yard.

— Annette M., 64, on her at-home experience

Does Annette's '50s lifestyle sound familiar? At first glance, it looks almost identical to mine. As an at-home mother who has lived through the feminist revolution, I might be tempted to think that the more things change, the more things stay the same. Perhaps the script has already been written for at-home mothers: check local listings for *Leave It to Beaver* reruns.

Not so, though. Get below the surface similarities and you will find a world of difference between the beliefs and attitudes and assumptions that underlie Annette's lifestyle and those that underlie today's at-home mother's lifestyle. Annette told me that she and her husband never had, never could have, discussed the possibility of her working outside the home. In most cases, at-home motherhood was the *only* choice, regardless of the personal preference of the woman. This meant that a significant portion of Annette's generation felt frustrated and limited, just as Betty Friedan described them in her landmark work, *The Feminine Mystique*. By contrast, today's woman is making a free and conscious choice.

Getting Organized

This book is organized into three parts. Part One, "Relationships," focuses on defining and developing your roles as a mother, wife, friend, and member of the community and the greater society. Part Two, "Business Matters," details ways to handle practical concerns including financial planning, smart shopping, and housework. Part Three, "On Your Own," forms the heart and soul of the book, concentrating on the self-development of the at-home mother.

If a self-help book is to have any value, the reader must actively participate in as well as take in information; otherwise, no real change occurs. Therefore, each chapter has a section or sections in workbook format. After reading the material presented in each chapter, you will have the opportunity to work through a series of guided questions and activities in which you can apply the concepts presented in the reading to your own situation. This process will enable you to realize the greatest benefits from the book. I suggest you write down your responses. Writing down thoughts not only clarifies and focuses thinking, it strengthens the force of these thoughts so that you can more easily translate them into reality. It also allows you to review your work, reevaluate your answers, and determine your progress in achieving goals.

Mindful that at-home mothers don't get much uninterrupted time, I've broken down what I have to say into small chunks and concentrated the information as much as I could. Read the book and work on your own or, better yet, use it as a kitchen table book that you and a group of other at-home mothers work through together.

At-Home Motherhood: Making It Work for You is unabashedly for and about at-home mothers. Using this book as a compass to guide you on your journey, you will be prepared for the inner and outer challenges you will encounter along the way. It can help you to redefine yourself with new missions, activities, interests, affiliations and relationships. I hope to encourage you to perceive yourself as a woman for whom parenting is only one part of your life's work. But while you are involved in it, it is the most important job in the universe. You've made the right choice to devote yourself to it.

2

A Sense of Mission at Home Full-Time

> They have only stepped back in order to leap farther.
> — Montaigne[1]

Why do women with years of career experience leave the working mainstream to stay home with children? The answer to this question usually involves five separate but interrelated missions:

- ✔ They want to raise their children in a less stressful environment.

- ✔ They want to be their children's primary caregivers.

- ✔ They want both quantity and quality time with their families.

- ✔ They want to be their children's first teachers.

---

[1] As quoted in John W. Gardner and Frances Gardner Reese, *Know or Listen to Those Who Know* (New York: W. W. Norton & Co., 1975), 200.

✔ They want to enjoy the pleasure of their children's company.

We will explore these five missions in the following pages.

Insuring the Domestic Tranquility

Maureen, formerly a successful graphic artist with a prestigious ad agency in New Orleans, is now mothering her two pre-schoolers full-time. She calls herself a "retired workaholic." She jumped off the Superwoman treadmill because she found the realities of dealing with two missions—career and childrearing—at the same time to be an impossible task. Maureen's story is a common one. Many women cite the stresses of trying to do it all—the inevitable work deadlines, impossible scheduling, the physical and mental strains and stresses—as the primary reason for heading home.

David Elkind, in his thought-provoking book *The Hurried Child*, maintains that parents who work are under more stress today than at any time since the Great Depression. Overworked parents can easily become so preoccupied with the heavy demands put on them that they have little left over for the concerns of their children.

Many of us who have tried being Superwoman painfully recall days when we left our children in situations which we knew were not the best: We were too tired to make the calls and other complicated adjustments necessary to find better alternatives, or there was simply nothing better to be had. Memories of leaving Maggie and Anne at a daycare center I knew they hated still hurt the three of us ten years later. I, like many other stressed-out parents, took false comfort in the thought that children are resilient and can adapt to anything as long as they're loved.

Of course, being at home full-time doesn't guarantee that a mother will be accessible to her children. For example, a depressed at-home mother, preoccupied with her own problems, will have little enthusiasm for parenting. But it is also true that reducing the stress by doing one job instead of two substantially increases the probability that she will be able to meet her child's needs.

Many women have found that the peace of mind and domestic tranquility they gained by walking away from the workplace is well worth the price. Said one woman, "I miss the fun and the paycheck from working, but at night I feel at peace with things. That's worth a lot to me."

Opting for Mothercare, Not Othercare

Worries about the long-term effects of having our children cared for by a paid caretaker during our long daily absences are central to the choice of at-home motherhood. Can we really trust the person taking care of our child? The proliferation of sensational articles about molestation and abuse at daycare centers makes parents uneasy. Further, how is the child's ability to form emotional attachments affected when he or she rotates through caretakers at a center, or the caretaker has two other babies and three toddlers to care for, or one babysitter after another quits? Who will teach discipline, values, or even those little morals called manners, all of which take patience and intense one-on-one time? We know how angry and frustrated we feel when our beloved toddler is being a "pill" or the baby cries for hours, and we wonder how a sitter, who hasn't our love bond, feels. We also know that no one, no matter how kind and competent, can match our own enthusiasm and excitement over our baby's first step or first word or first questions.

Studies researching the impact of "othercare" make interesting reading but provide no hard and fast answers. Some studies link behavioral problems with absentee parents and indicate that children placed at daycare at an early age are less likely to be securely attached to their mothers. Other studies show that working women raise more independent children.

Case studies of psychologically wounded children of both working and non-working mothers abound. Rahima Baldwin, in her book *You Are Your Child's First Teacher*, effectively sums up the contradictory welter of research findings with this statement: "While studies have shown that ideal substitute care situations do no measurable harm to children, all situations are not ideal, and no studies show substitute care as being any better than any but the most abusive family" (128).

Some researchers claim children will be happy if their mothers are happy, working or not. The main character in the movie *This Is My Life* speaks to this point. One of her friends quotes this platitude in response to her concerns about all the traveling she is doing whereupon she replies that children don't care if their mothers are happy or not—they just want them to be there. If they were asked to choose between their mother in ecstasy in Hawaii or contemplating suicide in the next room, "they'll take suicide in the next room." In truth, children will be unhappy if their mothers are miserable, but the inverse does not follow. A happy mother, depending on what makes her happy, by no means guarantees a happy child.

What About Older Children?

Children don't automatically stop needing their mothers close by once they're over six. School-age children who were once relatively agreeable to daycare may now have their own opinions and be quite vocal in protesting their childcare arrangements. They may be burnt out with the on-site after-school daycare program or hate sitting home with a babysitter. What used to work when they were in kindergarten or first grade doesn't satisfy them anymore. In fact, many mothers maintain that the older children become, the more they need a supportive guiding force at home. Homework can easily become a source of frustration, especially when youngsters are working on their own. If Mother's not there, they are likely to spend the afternoon glued to the TV set or playing Nintendo until a parent arrives. Says Stephanie, who recently quit work to spend more time with her two school-age boys, "I spent more energy coordinating childcare for the 3 to 6 P.M. time slot than I did an eleven-hour day when they were 'contained' with one sitter. Besides, they're becoming interesting people and I want to participate more in their lives, not just manage them."

Even when the kids are out of grade school, you're still not home free. The sometimes frantic pace of teenagers is stressful. It helps to be relatively calm and relaxed whenever we handle the inevitable crises that come from having a teenager in the house. Making the social transitions to junior high and then to high school are traumatic for many children; taking on the heavier academic loads is also difficult. Left to ride the typical adolescent emotional roller coaster on their own, they might go off track. With no one home to talk to, they might then turn to friends for more peer guidance than they really need.

My daughter always asks me "Don't you trust me?" when I question her if she wants to just "hang out" after school with her friends. Yes, I trust her. But I still want to be on top of where she is, what she's doing, whom she's with, and when I can expect her home. As a former high school teacher, I'm aware of the steep rise in teenage suicides, drug and alcohol abuse and sexually transmitted diseases. I also know that even responsible teens need supervision in the afternoon and that empty houses are a prime set-up for sex, drinking alcohol, and abusing other drugs.

Putting in Time, Both Quality and Quantity

Home-based motherhood can't guarantee inner peace or successful, well-adjusted children, but it does usually guarantee more time with your children. Cardozo writes in *Sequencing* that an at-home mother does basically the same things with her children, such as discussing events of the day or sharing meals, that she would do if worked outside the home. But being with her children only two or three hours while they are awake instead of ten or twelve, "she would do only a fraction of the things she does, and she would do them without continuity" (155).

Most at-home mothers value the quantity and continuity of the time spent with their children. They believe that the quality of time is not a substitute for quantity. As Dr. Fitzhugh Dobson, the highly respected child-rearing expert, explains: Imagine that you are hungrily awaiting your order of filet mignon at a fine restaurant. When the order finally arrives, instead of a full-sized steak, you receive a lonely-looking square inch of the tenderest, finest section of the steak and a dab of gourmet potatoes. Would you be satisfied with the quality of the meal or would you want some "quantity" too?

Moreover, the overriding factor isn't just the child's need for the mother. Many women report that the their own longing to be there with their children pushes all other considerations aside. Knowing that childhood lasts an achingly short time, they don't want to miss out on these golden days. Furthermore, the old cliche is true: No one says on her deathbed she wished she had spent more time at the office; it's always, "If only I had spent more time with the family."

A word of warning. There is good news and bad news about being home with your children. The good news is that you and your pre-schooler will be together nearly twenty-four hours a day, day in and day out. The bad news is that you and your pre-schooler will be together nearly twenty-four hours a day, day in and day out. You will have days when you can't stand to be there, when your sense of mission goes out the door right along with your good temper. On those days you may agree completely with W. C. Fields when he said: Kids, yeah, I like kids...medium rare. But isn't that true of every job? And when it works, nothing in the world can match the satisfaction you will feel!

Teaching Our Children the Basics

All parents are their children's first teachers. However, full-time at-home mothers carry this responsibility to the ultimate degree. With no operating instructions to guide us and no formal qualifications to recommend us except love for our children, we take on the shaping of our child's character, personality and intellect. Day in and day out and in a thousand little ways, we transmit our own values, beliefs, attitudes, behaviors, and perceptions directly to them. Our children turn primarily to us for love, attention, guidance, reassurance, and information. We get to answer their first "whys": Why is the sky blue? Why do trees grow? Where do babies come from? The importance of what they learn in the home and through their relationship with us cannot be underestimated. Although we may be frightened at the immensity of the challenge, we still believe that the combination of one child, one interested parent, and time makes for an unbeatable teaching situation.

Teaching our children doesn't mean producing "perfect" children, precocious prodigies who play minuets, read novels, work the computer or swim laps by age three. It also doesn't mean hovering over our children to force daily learning sessions on them. We do, however, want to stay alert to those "teachable moments," which, I may add, don't wait until duly appointed "quality times."

Parenting expert Burton White maintains that "raising a bright 3-year old is much easier than raising a pleasant, unspoiled 3-year old" (90). Most of us have our hands full "just" trying to raise the reasonably pleasant and unspoiled variety, "just" knowing where they are and what they're doing so that we can provide supervision, attention, and support when they need it.

Given that the needs of young children change so rapidly, the best advice I can give you is this: Let your instinct for love and mothering guide you. Beyond that, invest in one or two good parenting books (see "Recommended Reading" at the end of this chapter), subscribe to a parenting magazine, or become familiar with the parenting section of your local library. By understanding how children develop, you can better encourage their growth; in so doing, you not only help your children but also enhance your own enjoyment and growth as a parent.

What follow are some ideas you might be able to adapt to your own "home school."

Routines

Children and mothers alike thrive on routines. Routines, the repetitive rituals of daily life, provide an inner structure for children that carries over into the school years, helping them cope with homework and other of life's pressures. Kissing Daddy goodbye in the morning; feeding the dog at a certain time; a bedtime routine of story, prayer, and then a "good night, sleep tight" provide a comforting order in a confusing grown-up world.

Teaching that there is a "time for everything"—a time to play, a time to pick up toys, a time to eat lunch, and above all, a time take a nap or go to bed—doesn't mean we become slaves to the clock. We are free to modify the routine at any time. Fortunately, as at-home mothers we have a unique opportunity to establish the routines we want established.

Guidance

"As the tree grows, so the twig is bent," goes the saying. Bending the twig involves more than years of "Do's" and "Don'ts" and the mastery of "time-out" techniques. Our own behavior as parents determines to a great extent how our children will behave; as the primary caregivers we are the main role models for our children. The fact that much of their teenage social behavior has its roots in our own behavior is sobering. As we guide our children's behavior, then, we should make a conscious effort to model positive behaviors.

A Stimulating Environment

A stimulating environment rich in learning opportunities is what we all want. Making the home as safe and accessible as possible so that our children are free to explore and investigate their world is a good way to start. Providing appropriate playthings is also important. Toys are not frills for children; they are their work tools. It's not necessary to spend a fortune on fancy or gimmicky toys that just add to the clutter. A few balls, a cardboard box, and some household items provide hours of playing pleasure. When purchasing toys, choose the basic time-tested items such as balls of all kinds, a sandbox with wet sand, doll houses, building blocks, Legos, an inexpensive tape recorder, tea party sets, and riding toys.

Because purchasing toys is a bit like baseball (you strike out more than you get a hit), consult your favorite parenting book for lists of age-appropriate toys. A little professional guidance can up your batting average. Here are a few toy-buying tips:

- ✔ Organize your child's toys so that all the parts to one toy are grouped together on a tray, shelf, or in a basket.

- ✔ Periodically go through the toy chest and remove and hide away a boxful of toys. On the next rainy day, produce this box of long-lost playthings and it will seem like Christmas all over again.

- ✔ Keep broken radios, clocks, and tape recorders so that your children can take (not smash!) them apart.

Language Development and Pre-Reading

As your children's first tutor in unraveling the mysteries of spoken and written language, you can do some things to help with the learning process.

✔ Spend time talking to your children, using simple language that they can understand. Make an effort to add new words and related ideas.

✔ Read aloud to your children. This is one of the best ways to prepare them for independent reading. As you read, help them find similarities and differences between the characters and/or items in the pictures.

✔ Read real (un-Disneyized) fairy tales to your age four and older children. Many child experts, notably Bruno Bettelheim, say that original fairy tales such as those by the Grimm brothers or Hans Christian Andersen provide particularly worthwhile reading material for children. The rich images and complex and subtle meanings feed the imaginations, souls and intellects of children while at the same time providing challenging and difficult reading.

✔ Spell out simple words with alphabet blocks or with magnetic letters on the refrigerator. This helps children make the initial connection between letters and words.

✔ Try labeling (with a piece of tape or stick-on labels) a child's special belongings and the place where they are kept. This method has been used successfully by first-grade teachers for years!

✔ When you're making a grocery list or writing thank you notes, let your child dictate ideas to you. You write down what he says, then show him the finished written product.

✔ After your child learns to read, keep her motivated by supplying books relevant to her interests. For example, if your child is a sports fan, subscribe to a sports magazine; if he likes to cook, check out a cookbook from the library.

✔ Limit television. Excessive TV viewing makes the mind lazy. When we read, we are required to produce mental images based on the words we see; when we watch the "boob tube," the images are ready-made.

Creativity

By encouraging our children's imagination through make-believe play and fantasy activities, we help our children develop the ability to think in images. This ability is a key component in creative thinking. Here are some ideas:

✔ Keep a box of props that support make-believe productions, such as dress-up clothing, a suitcase, dolls, old eyeglass frames, wigs, stethoscope, and puppets.

✔ Start a "trash and treasure" box. Kids are natural packrats and notice all kinds of treasures that adults would throw away: old buttons, broken beads, egg containers, scraps of ribbon and fabric, milk cartons, wooden spools, cardboard tubes, seed pods, beans, pretty stones, gift wrappings and sacks. What to do with these treasures? Anything goes. Try making "interesting" greeting cards, bookmarks, jewelry, collages, mobiles, or even funny-looking robots out of glued-together items.

✔ Don't forget the ever-popular painting, gluing, craft-dough molding, singing and playing instruments as ways to teach creative self-expression.

✔ Play imaginary games with your child, using tea sets, doll houses and any number of toy sets that provide complete environments such as a farm, airport, etc.

The Natural World

Observing nature vicariously through the fresh eyes of a child is one of the more glorious aspects of motherhood. Expeditions to look at a beautiful tree, a perfect view, an interesting rock or a puddle full of bugs become major events. Some nature-loving ideas:

- ✔ Grow plants from seed and write down the changes your junior scientist observes as the plant matures.

- ✔ Try a different perspective on nature. Look closely at everything on the ground, or outline a circle on the ground and observe carefully everything within. Observe all the changes that occur over the period of a week. Lift up a rock or an old log and observe what goes on there. Watch the skies for cloud formations; gaze at the stars and point out the basic constellations.

- ✔ Get a magnifying glass. It will open up a fascinating new world for your child.

- ✔ Become bird watchers. Get a bird feeder and track the different birds that visit. Buy a tape of bird calls and learn to recognize the song of the bobwhite or the mourning dove.

Field Trips

We can beat cabin fever and provide new learning opportunities for our children by taking field trips. An excursion to the local fire station, police station, newspaper press, library, bakery, apple orchard, airport, or zoo will be more enriching and enjoyable than sitting the kids down for a snappy flashcard session.

Down Time

We all need time to relax and unwind. Remember, one of the main reasons you quit your job was to enjoy the freedom from routine and pressure. In your zeal to expose your child to a broad spectrum of activities, don't overschedule her into back-to-back lessons and activities. Children need free time just to daydream and to organize their experiences.

Just as your child is entitled to some time to himself, you are also entitled to some time away to do things on your own. Do yourself and your child a big favor and find a good sitter and use her services. You'll be a better parent for it.

Enjoying the Good Times

Good times go hand-in-hand with childhood. Good times set the stage for creativity, wide-open learning, and deep and lasting relationships. The sharing of these good times provides the stuff memories are made of. Giving a child a legacy of happy childhood memories is better than money in the bank; the warm feelings of being loved that are associated with the joy of special times provide a rich and solid account from which our children can draw strength and security as adults.

When I asked my teenage daughters what memories they treasured from their childhood, their response was interesting. They recited the usual litany of "the Christmas I got my first bike" and "the trip to Disneyland." But what they remembered the most were all those summer picnics at the pool. This was interesting because the grand and glorious picnics which apparently were the best of childhood times barely qualified as sack lunches. We nibbled on peanut butter and jelly sandwiches stacked up in a bread sack, carrot sticks in baggies, and drank a reconstituted lemonade drink from Dixie cups. But they enthusiastically recalled how much better these "samwiches," as they called them then, tasted in the great outdoors. They also reminded me of how I or one of my friends who ate with us usually produced a surprise of some sort—homemade chocolate cookies, fresh-washed strawberries dipped in powdered sugar or a Toblerone bar. At that moment I realized how happy I was to have shared those long, luxurious summer days with them year after year.

I was surprised at what an impression these rather ordinary lunches together had made. I took them for granted because we did it almost every day. Yet, I think it's the simple pleasures that we do regularly that make the best and most lasting memories for our children. While birthdays, class plays, the play-off game and graduations—big, one-of-a-kind events—are extremely important, they are only a piece of the pie. It's the ordinary things—planting flowers in the spring and watching them grow, taking little jaunts to the fruit and vegetable stand in the summer, making short visits to the nice neighbor who always gives out treats, baking cookies from scratch together—that shine like sunbeams in the mind of a child. Luckily, as at-home mothers, we have the time and energy to make most of them happen.

Here are some ideas for making a few sunbeams of your own:

✔ Go "parkhopping." Spend some time at the park noted for great climbing bars, then move to the one with the giant swings. Change venues for lunch so that you can dine alfresco in a wooded picnic area.

✔ Get physical with the kids. Let them "work out" as you exercise to an aerobic tape; let them bike or jog along with you when you go for a run. Take walks to interesting destinations where the kids can buy snacks; plan family hikes or bicycle outings. Play Frisbee or croquet, go rollerblading or iceskating, go swimming or run through the sprinklers, play tag or hide and seek. Play ball! Even the most unathletic can help a pre-schooler learn to throw a ball. Shoot baskets, kick the soccer ball, play catch and badminton. Ball games are definitely not just for dads anymore.

✔ Go on an air-conditioned "mall crawl" on a hot day when you want to beat the heat. Browse in the toy store, visit the animals in the pet shop, throw pennies in the fountain, and eat a frozen yogurt on a bench and watch the parade of people pass by.

✔ Stage a home drama or a fashion show in which you play a part.

✔ Let your kids organize a block party for the other kids in your neighborhood.

✔ Go fish. Even a pre-schooler can drop a line in the water. The only equipment it takes is a couple of poles, some bait, and a fishing license. The water is endlessly fascinating for children. Skipping or throwing rocks, catching water bugs and tadpoles with a net, and feeding ducks or fish will keep little ones happy even if they don't catch anything on their lines.

✔ Let your children create the meals, not just consume them. Children, like sharks, are naturally attracted to food. As long as you limit the "ammunition," their stirring and mixing and measuring can do little harm and can do a great deal in terms of family fun.

✔ Vow to spend a few minutes each day doing something special with your kids, even if it's just playing with the family cat, singing a few songs together or playing a quick game of Chutes and Ladders.

Exercises for Developing Your Mission Statements

While this material is still fresh in your mind, we will work through some questions that will help you develop mission statements about your role as an at-home mother. Take a blank sheet of paper (the first of many you'll be using as you work through this book) and focus on what you want to accomplish at home. Think about what you want to give your children that you couldn't give them if you were employed full-time.

1. Think back to your own childhood. What things did your mother do that you loved or that really made a difference in your life? List at least three.

2. What things did your mother do that you would like to do differently? List at least three.

3. Think about notable mothers you know. What do these women do that you might want to make one of your own missions? Write down three.

4. List at least ten goals you would like to accomplish during your time as an at-home mother. Here are a few guidelines:

   a. Let your ideas flow. This is brainstorming, not English 101. No one will read your mission statements but you, so don't sweat the grammar and spelling. There are no right answers.

   b. Make your statements "I"-oriented and active. In other words, don't make your mission dependent on others doing something for you. For example, "I want to raise a daughter who can support me and care for me in my old age" speaks more about what your daughter's mission is rather than your own. Another bad example would be, "I want to get my husband to be a Little League coach." You have no control over his choice to be or not to be a coach; try instead, "I will get more involved with my son's physical fitness by volunteering to be the assistant soccer coach on his team."

c. Make your statements concrete. Instead of saying, "I want to start having fun with my kids," say, "I want to plan at least one fun activity a week with the kids." Instead of saying, "I want to raise nice kids," say, "I want to work on table manners every day." Testing specific objectives will make it easier to see what steps you must take to accomplish them.

5. Now that you have a list of at least ten mission statements, read through the list carefully. Are there any repeats? Are any so similar they could be combined?

6. From your list of ten, pick the five that are the most important to you. This doesn't mean you aren't going to accomplish the others, but if you have too many goals, your attention will be spread too thin. It's better to concentrate your energies on the "biggies" first. Write down the five finalists for later reference. In the last chapter of this book, I will give you a technique for breaking down these goals into small, manageable steps that you can tackle one at a time. Refer to these mission statements whenever you're feeling like throwing the baby out with the bathwater. Don't throw away your brainstorming sheets. They're brimming with constructive thinking. Read your words, and their power will lift you up when you are feeling down.

Recommended Reading

Baldwin, Rahima. *You Are Your Child's First Teacher.* Berkeley, California: Celestial Arts, 1988.

Brazelton, T. Barry. *Toddlers and Parents.* New York: Delacort Press, 1974.

Dobson, Fitzhugh. *How to Parent.* Los Angeles: Nash Publishing Co., 1971.

Jones, Molly M. *Guiding Your Child from Two to Five.* New York: Harcourt Brace, 1967.

Leach, Penelope. *Your Baby and Child from Birth to Age Five.* New York: Alfred A. Knopf, 1978.

White, Burton. *The First Three Years of Life.* New York: Prentice-Hall, 1985.

3

Mixing Marriage and At-Home Motherhood

Since I started staying at home with the kids, Joe and I
are much closer. Instead of being on parallel tracks,
we're more like a jigsaw puzzle: we fit together.
— Karen, thirty-nine-year-old mother
of two pre-schoolers

At-home motherhood changes a marriage relation-
ship, often for the better. As mentioned earlier, most of today's
married couples truly choose this lifestyle, unlike their grand-
mothers and grandfathers who had the choice made for them.
As a result, most modern women don't feel trapped at home
and their husbands don't feel put upon by the responsibility
of being the sole breadwinner. Because working outside the
home is always an option once the children are out of the home,
at-home motherhood is not a choice partners have to live with
forever if they don't want to. Chances are, you will be at home
for just a season of your life. Savor it as the once-in-a-lifetime
experience that it is.

Like Karen and Joe, many couples experience a deepening of respect and love and trust in this more traditional arrangement. The added flexibility and time that come with at-home motherhood provide the loving attention and nourishment that allow a marriage relationship to blossom.

These days, for thirty-six-year-old at-home-mom Martha, the high point of the day is the evening spent with her husband: "Sometimes I feed the kids early so Jim and I can have a nice dinner together. We share news of the day, our little triumphs or failures, interesting tidbits from the paper, plans for the future, and best of all, new ideas. It's the kind of intimate fun we used to have when we were dating—not just the routine business stuff like arranging to take the car into the shop, which was typical dinner fare when I was working. All in all, it's a good way to live."

However, new challenges go hand-in-hand with this new lifestyle. In this chapter we will examine the new roles you and your husband play and the potential problems in adjusting to these roles. Lastly, we will take a look at suggestions for successfully mixing at-home motherhood and marriage.

The Concept of Interdependence

Perhaps you and your husband embrace at-home motherhood enthusiastically, seeing it as a great adventure in a lifetime of many adventures. If so, you both understand that this lifestyle is based firmly on the concept of interdependence. Interdependence in marriage means that both you and your husband agree that at this point in your family lifecycle, your chief contribution is taking care of the needs of the family and creating a homelife while his is supporting the family financially. Further, both of you understand that your husband's career and your care of the family are of equal importance; both are essential. In this way you can operate your family as a self-sufficient unit.

It is vital for you to understand your position in the marriage within the context of interdependence. Within the context of interdependence, you can avoid feeling like you are reverting back to "the little woman to his big man" model of days past which contemporary consciousness rejects as demeaning. Interdependence is a bigger concept than just dividing up the work. It means each partner is working hard to discern and fulfill the needs of the other. Depending on each other does not mean that you are dependent in the clingy, helpless sense. The concept of interdependence promotes the dignity, power and love of all family members and does so at no one's expense.

This is the ideal. Most couples don't start out so smoothly. Most go through a period of personal growth before this picture of interdependent harmony comes into focus. Intellectually we may know how the picture should look, but our emotions tell a different story.

Mixing marriage and at-home motherhood involves complex issues. What is your husband's reaction to his new role? Are there hidden assumptions about housework and parenting? Will you and your husband have trouble bridging the gap between the two separate worlds of work and home? What are the pitfalls? What can you do to ease the transition? Let's take a closer look at these issues.

Your Husband's New Role As the Sole Breadwinner

Many men don't feel the same pull to be with their children as women do. Furthermore, the responsibility for the children's care is traditionally the wife's, whether or not she works outside the home. You can probably remember being surprised, as I was, at how breezily some husbands can kiss their children goodbye in the morning, head out the door, and not give a second thought to the kids until they return that night. Because most husbands aren't anxious about their children in the first place, having a wife at home does not reduce any anxiety in that regard.

What is reduced is the family income—a frightening prospect, especially in these tough economic times. Although on the surface your husband may support the change, he may surprise himself and you with the negative feelings that surface when his new role as the sole breadwinner becomes reality.

First of all, some husbands become anxious about the reduction in lifestyle. They don't find it as easy to wave good-bye to a major portion of their family income as they do to their kids at the daycare center. It hits especially hard if a husband has a commission-based or seasonal income, which fluctuates radically from month to month and year to year.

Secondly, a husband may think his wife is copping out. He may have thought he and his wife started marriage with a conscious (or unconscious) agreement to be a dual-income family. When his wife quits a job to stay home, it may seem like changing the rules in mid-game. From his point of view, she has stepped off the fast track, escaped all job pressures, and considers every day to be Saturday. "So much for pulling the same load," he may grumble.

Finally, a career is often a man's top priority; everything else in his life revolves around it. On the other hand, once a woman has a baby, her career usually becomes less of a priority for her. A husband may be thrown off by this surprising turnaround in his wife's attitude. For that matter, so can she.

What You Can Do to Ease the Transition

✔ Listen to and try to understand your partner's concerns without overreacting. Maintaining open communication lines is the key to helping him overcome this hurdle. His reaction is perfectly normal; people frequently find unexpected gaps between what they think and how they feel. The fact that he agreed in the first place means that he does sincerely believe in the plan; it's just that the reality is more painful than he had anticipated. Understand that this lifestyle choice does, in fact, demand great sacrifice and maturity on his part.

✔ Don't change the plan. Understanding your husband's sudden cold feet does not mean reversing the course of action that you both have determined is best for the family. This is an opportunity for you to assume leadership. One tongue-in-cheek definition of leadership is "the ability to make others go along with what they don't want to do." Ultimately he'll thank you for helping him stick with the program.

✔ Tell him how much you admire him for the ambition, persistence and courage he has put into his work. Express your gratitude for the good things in life his working earns.

✔ If he feels like Atlas, carrying the whole world on his shoulders, give him a positive way of seeing your new relationship. Help him to understand the concept of interdependence and to accept the idea that you are doing your share by providing a secure family structure and home life.

✔ Reassure him that you're not backing off paid work forever. This is just for a season. Children do grow up and go to school; wives do reenter the workforce. Point out other sequencing women you know who have gone back to work.

✔ Address his worries about money. Plan together how to keep expenses down and then follow through on the plans.

✔ Give yourself time to adapt to your new role. Don't come to any drastic conclusions about yourself or your mate during this transition time. Realize that many difficulties are only temporary.

Fathering and At-Home Motherhood

Some fathers see their role in a different light once their wives are at-home full-time. Now, when they bathe the children or get up at night with the baby, it's a favor.

Active involvement with the children is an important part of fathering, and you're only *mothering* at home full-time. In short, he's not off the hook. Reading to the children, bathing them, or getting up at night to change a wet baby before the midnight feeding are part of good fathering regardless of whether you are there all day or not. The old stereotype of fathers who come home, read their paper, kiss the kids goodnight and then disappear into their studies to watch TV is no longer acceptable.

But there are those husbands who refuse to help. If you're in this situation, try to negotiate standards of behavior that involve him in daily interaction with the children. Make sure that when your husband does take responsibility for a job, you don't criticize him unnecessarily. For example, if your husband changes the diapers but they're too loose to suit you, make no comment. With practice, he'll get it right. Don't give up. People do change, but not overnight. Remember, only babies like a change. Start in small ways, giving plenty of encouragement. Negotiate for evenings out—he plays basketball with his friends one night a week and you take a class at a local college on a different night. This will give him the opportunity to take over the household and, more importantly, to interact with the kids.

Housework and Husbands

Today's woman who makes a conscious choice to stay home knows she will have to make changes and compromises. "I'm not at home to have sparkling toilets. I'm here to create a stimulating environment for our children," says Joanna of her life with her two grade-schoolers. "Although I do end up with the bulk of the cleaning just because I'm there." Like Joanna, today's at-home mom often ends up with most of the menial jobs on her "to do" list, but not because it is "woman's work"; rather, the housework detail was a trade-off she made in order to stay home full-time. She knows menial tasks are as much her husband's domain as hers.

Today's at-home mother has four basic choices regarding housework:

1. Do it all and take pride in it.

2. Be a "housekeeping minimalist" who does what absolutely has to be done and ignores the rest. The floor doesn't have to be clean enough to eat off if you eat on a table.

3. Negotiate with your husband to share household responsibilities. If you hate to clean the shower stall but like to prune bushes, maybe you can switch.

4. (The dream choice:) Hire it out.

If a mother has any free time (she may have none when children are very small), she does not expect to use it doing discretionary dusting and waxing. Moreover, she recognizes the truth in Phyllis Diller's statement: "Cleaning a house with small children is like shoveling the driveway during a snowstorm." We at-home mothers recognize that we have the right and the need to get out of the house on a regular basis. We must develop ourselves as separate individuals, and that requires time away from the home and, by extension, from housework. Therefore, we need to communicate our housework preferences to our husbands so that they too can set realistic expectations.

In spite of all the reasons not to become overly tidy, we may still feel guilty that our house is less than perfect. We may feel the need to justify our existence by raising our standards in the laundry room or in the kitchen even though we had intended to have a comfortably messy home. After all, our family did promise to learn to live with clutter. One aspect of this unexpected urge to justify our existences through housecleaning is illustrated by what my friend Tina calls the Red Alert Syndrome.

Tina relates how at her house at 5 P.M. (an hour before her partner, Rich, is due home) the disheveled kitchen with toys strewn across the floor and the messy bathrooms with towels askew and smudges on the mirrors start looming large in her mind. She then announces the call to action: "Red Alert." The kids know the drill. They scramble to their feet, take plates and glasses to the kitchen, and throw Legos and baseball gloves into their closets. Meanwhile, Tina quickly vacuums the carpets and Windexes the kitchen counters. "You might think that Rich is some kind of an ogre. He's not. He just wants the house to be basically picked up, nothing fancy."

I think a certain amount of "red alert" houseprimping is good. It shows pride in your home and respect for your husband. However, if you overfunction in this regard, your "red alert" behavior can become irrational and may need to be curbed. For example, on days when you've been home all day nursing sick children, acute anxiety about a messy house is inappropriate. You should feel comfortable asking your husband to pitch in to help pull things together. Roseanne Barr, queen of the comfortable look, rationalizes her messy house in this way: "Hey, the way I figure it is this. If the kids are still alive by the time my husband comes home, I've done my job."

For more about housework, see chapter 6.

Our Money

Many women feel uncomfortable with the financial dependence at-home motherhood brings. They don't think they are earning their keep. They may feel like maternal mooches living off his earnings. Some feel so guilty spending "his" money that they hide receipts and other records of money spent on non-essential items. Again, we may know in our minds that our husbands earn an income that is ours just as we are raising children and running a household which is ours. However, that money still seems like his.

Some women experience not earning money as a loss of personal power. The cynic's Golden Rule—"He who has the gold, makes the rules"—may seem too close to the truth. Believing this may cause it to become a self-fulfilling prophesy. Having joint bank accounts and possibly an account of your own can help ease this situation. See chapter 7 for suggestions regarding working out financial matters with your husband.

Staying Close in Separate Worlds

My friend Phyllis' husband used to call once or twice a day from work just to chat, even when he had no real reason to do so. As this was not the norm in my marriage, I asked her about it. She said her husband calls frequently because "the office is such a pressure cooker, a phone call to home puts him in touch with 'a different world' and he liked that."

Living in two different worlds, the world of work and home, can work for a couple, not against them. Vive la difference. You may be fascinated by office politics and glimpses into the lives of people whom you hardly know except for the five minutes at the Christmas party. Your husband, on the other hand, may treasure the window on his children that you offer, especially when they are too young to talk for themselves.

Staying close requires maintaining interest in each other's lives. This is largely tied to you as a person. It is your ability to

35

be a sensitive listener and to keep your self-confidence that keeps you in touch. One of the main purposes of this book is to help you find ways to keep growing emotionally and intellectually so that the inner richness you develop will keep you interested in life and make you more interesting as a person.

If you have difficulty maintaining your self-confidence, you may experience problems within your marriage. Next, we'll examine some of these potential traps.

Overvaluation of Your Husband

Women who overvalue their husbands (and devalue themselves) often think: "He's so smart. I could never do that" or "If I were supporting us, we'd be out in the streets." If you are beginning to believe that because he's working and you're not, all the power and ability in the family streams over to take up residence in his body, then he will indeed become the last word on every issue. You, the now powerless person, will begin to anticipate his reactions and assume you know what his thinking on any subject involving you will be. You will begin to structure your life around, "He wouldn't like it if I did that." The sad part is, you may never test your assumptions to see if they're accurate. If a woman believes in what she wants and acts decisively to get it, more things are possible than she thinks.

Uneven Development

If a woman allows her reservoir of self-esteem to fall dangerously low, she may withdraw into her own home and into her children's lives to the point where she has no life of her own. She now sees herself as "just a housewife," a drudge and a bore.

Forty-five-year-old Mary recounts those painful days of her first marriage. She resented her husband's freedom to roam the world as an executive with a large high-tech corporation, staying at fine hotels and dining in five-star restaurants. She was jealous of all the glamorous and sophisticated women she imagined him working with. "I even resented his growing self-confidence and his new ease with people. As he became more worldly, I became more frumpy and provincial—or that's how I saw it." Mary would desperately count the loads of laundry she did each day so that at dinner she would have something to report. Gradually they began to dread vacations and other times when the children were gone. They eventually divorced, no longer having anything in common as a couple.

No matter how busy we are with the children, we should never let our husbands think they rank second in our affection and concern. And no matter how involved husbands are with developing a career, they have a responsibility to help their wives find ways to grow along with them. Uneven development can be avoided if marriage partners commit themselves to help and support the other in his or her growth as an individual. One should never have to sacrifice one's self-esteem in a marriage relationship.

Communication Breakdown

Parents of newborns are particularly vulnerable to losing touch with each other. Couples who previously worked out conflicts over a glass of Chianti in an Italian restaurant now, since the birth of their baby, fall asleep right after dinner. They are too tired to even talk about their differences, much less do something about them.

Charles Osgood's lead-in to his January 7, 1993, morning newscast, "The Osgood File," hit the nail on the head: "What word begins with "S," has one syllable, takes place in a bedroom, and is something that most Americans can't get enough of?" After a long pause came the answer: "Sleep." Few parents are prepared for the fatigue that sets in with the arrival of a baby or for the amount of time that just feeding a baby takes. At first sleep may assume priority over time for your spouse.

A period of adjustment is normal after a birth. However, if a couple continues to neglect their own relationship, eventually the marriage may drift. The magical circle of family closeness will never develop; instead the circle will break apart.

Bob and Arlene are headed in this direction. After the birth of their children, Arlene quit her job and tried to adjust to her new status. Meanwhile, Bob would come home from a hard day at the office, feeling tired and irritable and not looking forward to another night of interrupted sleep. "The house would be a mess," Arlene recalls. "Although I tried to explain how hard it was to keep a clean house with a toddler and an infant, he would look around and say, 'What did you *do* all day?'"

Bob seemed to lose interest in her. She in turn lost interest in preparing dinners when he began arriving home at unpredictable hours. "Eventually we just stopped talking," Arlene sighs, "and he'd just come home, watch TV and fall asleep." When she suggested going out for a movie and dinner, Bob refused and replied that he was too tired. "Well," Arlene concluded, "I was tired too, but I desperately needed his company." Bob and Arlene eventually went to a therapist to see if someone could help them start communicating again.

Keeping the home fires burning brightly can be difficult when separate worlds and sleep deprivation get in the way. What follows are suggestions that will help you keep the lines of communication open.

- ✔ Make a pact to talk about your feelings. Set aside some time each night in which you and your mate take turns talking about what you are feeling—not what you did all day. After you've stated clearly and lovingly how you feel about a subject, ask him "How do you feel about that?" Then be ready to listen to his answer. Don't be afraid to disclose angry or negative feelings as long as you do it lovingly. Admitting such feelings can bring great relief.

- ✔ Use "I" and "me" statements when you talk. For example, say, "I sometimes feel resentful when I have to clean up the dinner dishes by myself night after night." This is less threatening than, "You don't do anything around here anymore."

✔ Keep in mind that men and women communicate differently. Generally, women feel more comfortable talking about feelings than men do. Sitting across the kitchen table, maintaining constant eye contact and talking about feelings is something men rarely do. However, they are more likely to open up in the context of a shared activity like raking leaves or going on a walk or drive.

✔ Remember that in conversation women usually go from the general to the specific; men go from the specific to the general. Therefore, if you're opening a conversation about how you think the two of you are neglecting your relationship (actually you think he's mostly doing the neglecting) and need more time together, don't start with this idea. Instead, talk about a specific activity you would like to do as a couple, and based on his reaction, lead back to the general concept.

✔ Cuddling, stroking, kissing and hugging are not just for babies. Being physically affectionate with your spouse can set a warm, close tone for other areas of your relationship.

✔ Adopt a problem-solving approach to difficulties. Define the problem in specific terms and develop solutions together.

✔ Find a sitter or a co-op for every Saturday night and go out on a "date" once a week. If another couple invites you out to dinner or you have a family get-together, don't count that as a date. Reschedule for Wednesday. Spending time with groups is important but it doesn't take the place of a one-on-one talk between the two of you. If you worry that you won't have anything to talk about, see a movie first.

✔ Don't forget the great lesson of feminism: every woman should continue self-development throughout her lifetime. This will pay great dividends in terms of your marriage in the long run. (Part Three is devoted to your personal development.)

✔ Tell you partner you love him, both in words and in how you treat him. Keep the words of Theodore Hesburgh in mind: The most important thing a father can do for his children is love their mother. The reverse is equally true.

Exercises for Mixing Marriage and At-Home Motherhood

1. In the space provided, write "T" for "True or "F" for "False" in response to the following statements:

_____ I maintain a daily interest in my husband's work and make an effort to keep straight the names, problems and job politics he tells me about.

_____ My husband and I have made our marriage a priority above our relationship with our children.

_____ My husband and I spend time alone each week.

_____ My husband and I openly discuss our feelings about house rules for the children, spending, housework, and standards and values.

2. Think back to when you were dating. What sorts of things did you do then that you would like to

do more of now? Write down three activities you could reinstate into your relationship.

3. When do you and your husband talk the most (in the car, when you're out for dinner, after the kids go to bed)? Build in those situations and consciously use that time for talking.

4. List three things you could do to help your husband get more enjoyment out of his new role.

5. List three little things you could do to improve the quality of the time you and your husband spend together.

6. How do you and your husband split up household and parenting responsibilities? Are you happy with this arrangement? What would you like to change?

7. What unrealistic expectations about marriage and parenting do you have, if any?

8. What do you think your husband's three biggest worries are? Ask him and see if you are right.

9. What do you think your three biggest strengths are as a wife? Ask your husband what he thinks they are and compare.

10. Now list your husband's three greatest strengths as a husband. Ask him what he thinks they are and once again, compare.

4

In the Company of Women

"Jane, how long was Ryan sick with that flu? Because
last night..."
"...and she said editing at home is a good way to earn
extra money..."
"...Where did you say you saw kids' sneakers on sale?"
"Well, time to go. (*Laughing*) We've got to stop meeting
like this."
— Three mothers in the nursery school parking lot

After kissing our toddlers goodbye, we linger in the
parking lot, dressed in our uniform of sweats or jeans and
relishing our "freedom." We animatedly exchange news bul-
letins for ten minutes, then break up reluctantly to start our
daily round of errands.

I have thought to myself that women should never stop
"meeting like this," meaning in unglamorous spots like parking lots, crowded grocery store aisles, the muddy sidelines of
soccer fields, or on busy street corners as we hang out of vans
large enough to house the 49ers. It's tough with small children
around to squeeze in time with our peers. Yet it's even tougher

to survive without the contact, so we become versatile about details such as dress code and meeting places.

Women at home who have a strong reinforcing community of friends are far happier in their roles than women who don't. Thus, it's important to commit the time and energy for friendships. Let's take a closer look at five big reasons why friendships assume such importance for us.

The Importance of Friends

Friends Counteract Isolation

One of the most difficult hurdles at-home mothers encounter is loneliness. Debbie, a five-year veteran of at-home motherhood, recalls that the long days spent completely alone without other adults to talk to took her by surprise. Says Debbie, "I was so starved for company, I literally counted the minutes until my husband got home." It's easy to start feeling cut off from the world when you're absorbed with an infant, who, when she's not clamoring for your attention, sleeps and eats away most of the day. Sometimes the quick fix of laughter and support you get from a phone call with a friend is enough to turn around a sagging attitude. Debbie adds, "I make it a point to call at least one friend every day."

Friends Can Help You Build a New Life

William James once said that wherever you are, it is your own friends who make your world. When we are adjusting to staying home full-time, we may feel disconnected from our old world of workfriends who may not even know the right questions to ask someone who spends her day changing diapers. We require a new world of friends who can commiserate with what's on our minds right now and can help us build a new life that features children.

Lee, twenty-nine, recalls the period right after the premature birth of her first son. Her husband was trying to prove himself at the New York law firm he had just joined and was often on the road four nights out of seven. That left overwhelmed Lee alone to cope with their colicky, demanding baby while she herself tried to recover from serious birth complications. Then she met her neighbor Betsy, an experienced mother with two grade-school sons. As they got to know each other, Betsy helped Lee find Dot, a loving, reliable babysitter, so the two of them could enroll in exercise class and go out to lunch and shop periodically. She also helped Lee get involved in a woman's group at her church.

Betsy brought not only her freshly baked bread and the world's best Italian meatballs to Lee's door but also her sense of adventure. With Matthew in his Snuggli, they explored exotic markets together and went on nature hikes. As Lee puts it, "She helped me get a life." Lee's health gradually began to improve as did her strained relationship with her husband, Joe. Because she was building a new life of her own with Betsy, she didn't resent Joe's long absences from home as much. "All it takes is one friend—you don't need dozens," remarks Lee.

Friends Provide Affirming Role Models

Notable at-home mothers like Betsy, whose unexpected acts of kindness touch our lives, can serve as role models as we grow and develop at home. Through their example, we stretch our own perception of what we are capable of at home. These so-called "ordinary housewives" do extraordinary things for us. They may help us out with childcare when we suffer a death or hospitalization in our family. But more often than not, they do little everyday things: bail us out of an impossible scheduling snafu or nurse our children sent home sick from school until we get home. Just as important, they offer words of praise and encouragement when we're having trouble coping.

Over time, the sum of all these offerings of friendship amount to an extraordinarily great gift of love. We never forget these special role models who were there for us at critical points in our lives. Sometimes, only when she is at home full-time does a woman discover how wonderful women can be, especially if she is used to thinking of other women as office rivals. By perceiving this greatness in women who are also at-home mothers, we affirm the potential for greatness in our own lives and in ourselves.

Friends Provide Emotional Support

"My friends are my therapy," is an oft-heard comment among mothers, and for good reason. First of all, women are usually attentive listeners. Unlike men, who tend to be more results-oriented and want to get to the point quickly in order to find immediate solutions, women are more process-oriented. They allow you to talk freely, to rehash the details and nuances of a situation without forcing a solution. And sometimes this is really all you need—a sympathetic ear. One woman commented that with friends like this, who needs a perfect husband?

Second, like therapists, friends help us process events of the day or week to gain a new understanding of them. One woman joked, "I can leave the house convinced I'm the only mother who 'loses it' with a son who I half fear is borderline psychotic. After an hour of 'therapy' with my friends, I can see my situation for what it is: my son's behavior is normal for an independent, high-spirited ten-year-old. And my yelling at him is normal too."

Finally, sometimes you don't have to say anything to feel the therapeutic effects of friends. Simply by listening to and helping others, we regain our perspective. As one woman said of her friends, "We're both caseload and caseworker to each other in the never-ending battle to retain our sanity."

Friends Function As a Second Family

The average American family moves every five years. The at-home mother in that family will not only leave her hometown behind but will also bid goodbye to her extended family and a network of women friends. Her new neighborhood may be thousands of miles away and most of her new neighbors, including the women her age, are commuting to work by 8:30 in the morning.

Friendships with other at-home mothers and their families can relieve the loss of the real extended family, replacing it with what Betty Friedan calls "the extended family of choice." Friends can share birthday parties, piano recitals, Sunday afternoon barbecues, and holidays just as aunts, uncles and cousins would. A family of friends helps us feel more secure. We are part of a larger community and there is safety in numbers. Children also enjoy the feeling of security and continuity derived from relationships with dependable, caring adults who are interested in them and know them well.

Types of Friendships

An Inner Circle

Most women have an inner circle of one to five intimate friends. These friends with whom we share our innermost feelings and who are in touch with the details of our daily lives replenish us as we go about the sometimes draining business of nurturing others. Even though our husbands may be our "best friends," they often can't satisfy the need for day-to-day companionship that a close confidante or two can.

A Large Pool of Friends and Acquaintances

Beyond their inner circle, most women have a large pool of friends and acquaintances that includes neighbors, parents of children's friends and the many people they know through associations with playgroups, the PTA, sports, church, civic and political organizations and other special interest groups.

Within this pool the level of friendship ranges from a high degree of emotional sharing—the primary determinant of the level of friendship—to those "friends" with whom we have only a nodding acquaintance. These relationships are dynamic. For example, slight acquaintances can escalate into good buddies after you work shoulder-to-shoulder together on a long-term PTA project.

Women's Networks

Networking means getting together for the express purpose of accomplishing something. Usually this involves exchanging information, contacts, skills, tips, and moral support. Networking, an outgrowth of the women's movement, implies that just getting to know each other is not enough: a formal network with stated goals ensures that we get the help we need.

Literally thousands of women's networks have sprung up like mushrooms across the country to support mothers. Mothers' Workshop, a network that focuses on the special concerns of today's at-home mothers, and FEMALE (Formerly Employed Mothers At the Leading Edge), a support network that encourages mothers who left careers but will be returning to the workforce, are two examples of networks aimed strictly at supporting at-home mothers.

There are networks to help homeschoolers in their efforts to educate their own children, networks for mothers of premature babies, religious networks, and networks for ethnic groups and for spouses of physicians, military personnel, and clergypeople. The list is long and varied. The following list provides specific information regarding national networks geared for at-home mothers.

- ✔ **La Leche League International** supports mothers who breastfeed their babies. P.O. Box 1209, Franklin Park, IL 60131-8209, (800) LA LECHE or (708)455-7730

- ✔ **Formerly Employed Mothers At Loose Ends (FEMALE)** is a support and advocacy group for women who have interrupted careers to raise families. P.O. Box 31, Elmhurst, IL 60126, (708) 941-3553.

- ✔ **Moms Offering Moms Support (MOMS) Club** supports at-home mother of children of all ages. 814 Moffatt Circle, Simi Valley, CA 93065, (805) 526-2725.

- ✔ **Mothers of Preschoolers (MOPS)** is a Christ-centered support group for mothers of preschoolers. 4175 Harlan Street #105, Wheat Ridge, CO 80033, (303) 420-6100.

- ✔ **Mothers At Home, Inc.,** offers the newsletter *Welcome Home.* 8310 A Old Courthouse Road, (CT - A OLD?)Vienna, VA 22182, (703) 827-5903.

- ✔ **National Association of Mothers' Centers** offers Mothers' Center branches where mothers can come together to discuss concerns. 336 Fulton Avenue, Hempstead, NY 11550, (800) 645-3828.

- ✔ **Mother's Workshop** offers a newsletter that helps at-home mothers explore outside interests and strategies for tomorrow. P.O. Box 843, Coronado, CA 92118.

Family Resource Centers, found in most cities, offer parenting classes and other information useful to mothers. The only entrance "requirement" for joining a network is the desire to take part. You decide what's important to you and then locate groups with similar interests. Or, if you can't find one that suits your needs, start your own. You can form networks with other women through local community centers, YMCAs, churches, synagogues, and hospitals. Women's centers (also found in most large cities), community centers, churches, the local library and the local newspaper are good places to start.

Joining a network offers more benefits than providing much-needed information. If we have come home from a career, affiliating with a network is the fast track to filling in the identity gaps left by losing our former identities as bankers, teachers, or businesswomen. After I had Elizabeth, my youngest daughter, I joined a book club which met once a month in the evenings. This was just what I needed. We all shared a love of literature and a respect for each other's critical skills. Over the years I have become close friends with several members. But it is my membership in the group that I take particular pride in.

A network also provides accountability. Being our own boss is wonderful to a point, but some women may find they are less productive without the structure of a boss and deadlines to motivate them. A formal network provides this structure. After we share our ideas and plans, we know there will be someone at the next meeting who will check on our progress. This little extra "push" can make all the difference.

Playgroups

Playgroups are another popular form of networking for at-home mothers. A new twist on the old kaffeeklatsch tradition, playgroups meet once a week so mothers can talk with one another while their children play nearby. They meet in parks when the weather's good, at homes in cold or rainy weather, and periodically at the zoo, pizza parlor or beach.

Occasionally, the mothers get sitters and go out for a mothers-only breakfast. "We hardly recognize each other spruced up and without the bulging diaper bags we all schlep around," says Mary. Mary explains that one of the greatest things about her playgroup is the referrals she gets for everything from pre-schools and allergists to what tree surgeon to use. "Through my playgroup, I've saved many hours of research time. It's been my insurance against reinventing the wheel."

Most at-home mothers report that their playgroups mean a lot to them. Some playgroups fall apart when scheduling around pre-schools and naps becomes too complicated; others last. One woman I know still meets with her playgroup even though the toddlers have graduated from Big Wheels to real cars. Says Sue, "We meet for lunch once a month. We discuss whatever's on our minds—just like we did fifteen years ago when we were starting out."

How do you join a playgroup? Usually one or two mothers take the initiative. They call up other mothers with children in the same age group and organize a meeting time and place. Somebody volunteers to make up a list with phone numbers, addresses, and emergency numbers. If there aren't enough at-home mothers in your neighborhood, you can join groups from more distant areas. There may be an organization in your area that can help you find playgroups. For example, Las Madres is a Northern California network whose primary purpose is to organize neighborhood playgroups for mothers and children based on the child's date of birth. Or try contacting women's centers, churches, community centers and preschools to try to get connected.

Finding New Friends

If You Move to a New Area, Make Finding Friends a Priority

"Where you live is what you get" in terms of other moms at home during the day. Investing the time and energy into finding the right neighborhood full of moms and children on the same "mommy track" that you're on can pay tremendous dividends in terms of convenience and contentment for the whole family. In fact, finding the perfect house may be less important than finding the right neighborhood. It might be well worth the sacrifice of a spare bedroom or office.

Do some serious detective work to find out the real story. Asking your realtor is only the first step. Walk around the neighborhood between 4 and 6 P.M., when children are likely to be playing outside. Ring doorbells to inquire about where same-age children live and if their mothers work outside the home. Visit with kindergarten and pre-school teachers. A trip to the local library at storytime might put you in contact with at-home mothers who can give you an insider's view of various neighborhoods.

After you've decided on a neighborhood and are moving in, consider following the example of my friend Carol. The movers had barely finished loading their dollies and mats back into the moving van when Carol went knocking on the doors of all of her new neighbors, introduced herself, and invited them over. She seated her guests on boxes and served them coffee and doughnuts. She didn't have to go to any trouble and they loved getting to know her and chatting with their old neighbors whom they hadn't seen for a while.

Carol didn't take the usual two or three years to get connected in that neighborhood. She followed up her "getting to know me" coffee with frequent walks with her toddler. Along the way she stopped other mothers with strollers and introduced herself. She joined my playgroup and my jogging group, started singing in a church choir, and volunteered at her oldest son's pre-school. It wasn't long before she had a nice circle of friends and a network of acquaintances. Says Carol, "I still haven't met a soulmate like my best friend in Chicago. But I have found some good friends." Even if we're fortunate enough to land in a friendly neighborhood, we can't all hit the ground running the way Carol did, but we certainly can act on her premise that they won't come to us; therefore, we have to go to them.

At-Home Mothers Need to Systematically Seek Out Friends

At work you don't have to go out of your way to meet a pool of potential friends. But at home you will have to generate your own social life. You've got to "smile and dial" and get out there with people. Contact doesn't guarantee friends; however, lack of contact guarantees no friends at all.

Sometimes shyness holds us back. We don't want to appear overeager or needy. We may feel comfortable with the perfunctory and vague, "Let's get together for coffee sometime," but are not bold enough to follow through with a sincere invitation that demands a response. We don't like to risk rejection.

We have a natural tendency to assume that others are doing better in the friends department than we are. However, many times the women we assume to be so popular that they couldn't possibly be interested in us will actually enjoy our friendship if we give them the opportunity. You don't have to be a special person to make friends. Popularity, good looks and an outgoing personality are not prerequisites. What is required is a willingness to be a friend to others. Of course, not every invitation will get a positive response, but some will. Go ahead and make the phone call. If that fish doesn't bite, try another one.

Suggestions for Making and Maintaining Friends

✔ Don't feel guilty taking time for socializing. It's not a waste of time. You need this interaction. If you have come home from a career, think of it as part of your job to create the perks for yourself that were already built in for you when you worked outside the home.

✔ Volunteer. The more you do in your community, the greater your chances for meeting people. Sharing work promotes good conversation and mutual respect. This is often the best route for a truly shy person. The next chapter is devoted to how to become more involved in your community.

✔ Integrate your daily errands or exercise routines with social time with friends. For example, if you have to make a big haul at a discount food club, plan to go with your friend. Arrange for your and your friend's child to take ballet or swim lessons at the same time. Get a long cord or a cordless phone so you can visit with a friend while you fold laundry, unload the dishwasher or perform other "mindless" chores.

✔ Be a special events organizer. Everyone loves to participate, but not everyone will take the time to make the arrangements. If you plan to attend a lecture series or a children's play, ask a friend to join you. Scan the entertainment section for details about special events of interest to mothers and their children and put together a group. If the weather's nice, call two or three mothers and ask them to meet you for a picnic in the park. Organize a discussion group for at-home mothers.

✔ Be positive. This sounds trite, but it's basic to making and keeping friends. We are attracted to friends who bring out the best, most treasured parts of ourselves. We drive people away with chronic complaining or harsh criticism of others. On the other hand, if you're happy doing what you're doing and show it, others will enjoy your company.

✔ Expect the ebb and flow of friendship. We all need to pull back sometimes to allow ourselves or a friend some space.

✔ If a friendship is in trouble, analyze the cause. Apologize if you have hurt someone. If your friend has hurt you, let her know how you feel as clearly and lovingly as you can. If your friend has let you down in some way, remember that part of friendship is forgiving shortcomings. Sometimes we may strongly and persistently disapprove of a friend's actions. Perhaps she is having an affair or is taking advantage of you or someone else; perhaps she is a friend who never sets limits for her daughter yet suffers continually and angrily over the child's misbehavior in school. If the relationship can bear it, offer suggestions and hope the situation turns around. But if you see that she continues to create chaos in her own life or in others' lives through her actions, your ambivalent feelings may force you to withdraw from the relationship.

✔ Don't be afraid to request favors of your friends. In creating obligations to one another we bond more deeply. Ben Franklin's advice to be neither borrower nor lender doesn't hold true here as long as you return favors and borrowed goods in good shape and within reasonable amounts of time.

✔ Don't join the so-called "mommy wars" between mothers who work outside the home and at-home mothers. We need each other too much and have too much in common to regard each other as enemies. Can you remain friends with your working friends? Of course. As long as you keep up other interests besides the curing the baby's diaper rash or keeping the carpets clean, you'll find plenty to talk about. Your self-confidence is the biggest factor in how you relate to working women. If you're insecure about the value of your job at home, you may find time spent with former work friends distressing rather than rejuvenating. Bear in mind that many women's jobs are not glamorous, stimulating, or well paid. They probably envy you your freedom.

✔ Don't let treasured friends drift away. It takes a long time to grow an old friend, says writer

Elmore Leonard. Therefore, tend to them. If you both like basketball games or the theater, buy season tickets so you can sit together. Make a standing monthly date for lunch or dinner. Getting it on the calendar ups the chances for making it happen.

✔ Keep this oldie but goodie in mind: "You've got to be a friend to have a friend." Try to find ways to bring joy into friends' lives. Be available when your friends need you. When you're together, listen supportively and non-judgmentally. When your friend has a problem, try to guide her to her own conclusions. If necessary, help her find help. Don't be afraid to open up to your friends: Social facades are boring; the truth never is.

Exercises for Developing Your Friendship Mission

1. Who belongs to your inner circle? Could you use a few more close friends? If so, with whom would you like to become closer? List three strategies for getting to know them better.

2. What are your three greatest strengths as a friend? In what areas of friendship do you think you need improvement? List three things you can do now to be the friend you want to be.

3. What networks do you currently belong to? What networks would you like to belong to? What steps can you take to join?

4. Can you think of any unexplored opportunities for getting to know other at-home mothers? What can you do to start taking advantage of these opportunities?

5. Think of old friends who have drifted away. Are you content with the situation or would you like to see more of them? If the latter, what can you do about it?

6. Think of three nice "gifts of love" that you could offer to friends to show your appreciation for their friendship.

7. What steps could you take to be a better neighbor or to be a better substitute "aunt?"

8. Analyze how much time you spend making and maintaining friendships every week. Should friendship be higher on your priority list?

5

Reaching Out As a Volunteer

...Americans are more engaged in voluntary associations
and civic organizations than the citizens of most other
industrial nations.

—Robert Bellah[1]

T he "New Volunteerism" was officially ushered in by
George Bush in his 1989 "One Thousand Points of Light"
speech, in which he announced that "from now on, in America,
any definition of a successful life must include serving others."
Did he say "from now on?" we asked, looking up from our
room-mother calling lists. Evidently we at-home mothers have
been leading more successful lives than we realized.

American mothers have traditionally volunteered their
time at local hospitals, at their children's school, at their church
or synagogue. Unsung, unpaid, unselfish and unfazed by the
1980s culture, which dismissed volunteer work as naive, a vast
volunteer army of women has been working hard for the

---

[1] Bellah et al., *Habits of the Heart: Individualism and Commitment in American
    Life* (New York: Harper & Row, 1985), 163.

betterment of their communities. For them, serving others never went out of style.

Volunteer work has taken on a different cast in recent years. Volunteers still do the basics—organizing school Valentine's Day parties, selling raffle tickets for the church bazaar, working in the hospital gift shop. But today, after delivering the heart-shaped cookies and the canned punch for the class party, many volunteers roll up their sleeves to begin working out solutions to bigger problems. Government cutbacks in spending for education and human services have created desperate needs. Volunteers have stepped in to pick up where the money left off.

Public schools, where at-home mothers are most likely to be involved, are a case in point. In California, for example, budget cuts have forced school districts to drastically reduce personnel, services, and materials. As classrooms become more crowded, teachers are more overworked than ever. They must integrate non-English-speaking students into the mainstream while at the same time dealing with an ever-increasing number of students with learning and behavioral problems. What does this mean for those of us at home during the school day?

It means that in classrooms we tutor English, math and reading; we run art and music programs, often the first "frills" to go; we give the one-on-one instruction that many students desperately need. We work on programs for AIDS, drug and alcohol abuse and teen pregnancy, issues that didn't widely exist in the schools twenty years ago. Before and after school, mother-driven station wagons—not-expensive-to-operate yellow schoolbuses—transport students to and from school and sports activities.

Fund-raising efforts are strong and ongoing. Funds raised by volunteers pay for band directors, band uniforms, football equipment and even coaches. Volunteers raise money for everything from classroom computers to office copiers. We solicit businesses to sponsor classrooms the way they've sponsored sports teams in the past.

Needs are too great to rely strictly on old-fashioned fundraising techniques. The most effective fundraisers have gone professional. Volunteers employ sophisticated marketing and sales techniques and, of course, computers to persuade people to open their hearts and their pocketbooks. The old door-to-door campaigns are less effective now than they were in the '50s. Then, March of Dimes mothers canvassed door-to-door and raised millions of dollars to fight polio. Today, women in many neighborhoods are frightened to go door-to-door and the people behind those doors are afraid to open their homes to strangers.

It is precisely these professional and high-powered skills used in some areas of volunteer work that entice many women to donate their time. As we work in a nonpaid capacity, we can learn marketable skills which we can use later to find paid work. At-home mothers have always used volunteer work as an outlet for their creative and social energies, but now many of us keep our professional resumes in mind as we are deciding where to channel our efforts.

To be sure, we do reap certain personal benefits from volunteering, but the central focus of volunteer work—serving others—transcends self-interest. The old-fashioned ideals that have been the basis of the American altruistic tradition are still at the heart of volunteer efforts.

Five Ideals to Volunteer By

1. We have a moral obligation to extend a hand up and say, "Let me help you," to those who are in trouble.

2. When the institutions that serve our families and children are in trouble, we have a moral obligation to help. We can't depend on government to provide professionals to get the job done.

3. Much of what we are and what we have is due to social and cultural institutions we did not create ourselves. We owe a debt to society for these great gifts.

4. By our example, we want to teach our children the importance of the helping virtues: generosity, charity, compassion, tenderness, and unselfishness.

5. For many years while many of us were in the workplace, we depended on others to get the work done in the community. Now it's our turn.

I showed this list to a friend celebrating her sixty-fifth birthday. Knowing her to have been a consummate volunteer for most of those years, I was pleased she agreed that these ideals do indeed capture the deeper meaning that is at the heart of most volunteer work. Then she made an interesting comment. She said, "The fellowship you feel when you work together intensifies the meaning of the ideals that you all believe in—that's the real joy in it." She maintained that it is the sharing of these ideals with others that is the most significant factor in volunteer work. As we share the suffering and frustration of others who are pursuing the same idealistic goals, the meaning of those ideals is magnified.

So, how can we put these ideals into action?

Guidelines for Volunteer Work

Maximize the Good Feelings You Get from Giving

We've all heard that when you give, the good comes back to you. Often this is in the form of emotional satisfaction: feelings of self-confidence and mastery, optimism about life, human fellowship, inner peace and even joy.

It turns out that doing good helps you feel good in more than the emotional sense. According to Allan Luks' book *The*

Healing Power of Doing Good (New York: Fawcett Columbine, 1991), new research indicates a physical connection between doing good and feeling good. Helping others reduces stress by causing the release of the body's natural painkillers, the endorphins. He calls this physical sensation of well being the "helper's high." Luks also suggests that if we want to maximize good feelings, we should take the following four factors into consideration when choosing volunteer jobs:

1. Personal contact with the person you're helping is preferable to indirect helping as in collecting cans or clothes.

2. Frequent helping—Luk suggests a rough goal of two hours per week—is better than working on an annual fundraising event that involves two intense months of involvement, then ends.

3. Volunteering for a task that you are already equipped for, or will be trained to do, is obviously better than starting out blind.

4. Doing a job that is especially relevant to your interests will bring you the most satisfaction.

Schools Are a Good Place to Start

The degree of volunteer involvement in schools varies widely. Some mothers are highly selective about the work they do, preferring only to work on projects directly related to their own children. Others take on huge responsibilities, running complex policy-making committees with $30,000 budgets. There are three important reasons why involvement—great or small—in the schools is an almost universal experience for at-home mothers.

First of all, we gain a new window on our children's school experience, giving us a different view than from at home. We watch them interact with classmates and the teacher. We observe how they learn. We get to know their friends and often their friends' mothers. In this way, we can assess for ourselves the quality of their schoolday.

Secondly, if our children are having problems, we gain valuable information that we can use to develop strategies for helping them deal with each problem. For example, if our child comes home and complains that Johnny is picking on him, we might dismiss his complaint as an exaggeration. However, the next day, as we are tutoring in the classroom, we observe our child being verbally and physically abused by Johnny, the class bully. Armed with this firsthand knowledge of the situation, we can support our child appropriately.

A similar but more unusual dynamic involves observing the teacher. Although most teachers are excellent, occasionally a teacher unknowingly undermines the teaching process or may even damage a child's self-esteem. In this case, it would be good to be involved in a capacity where you have firsthand information, access and input.

Thirdly, by getting involved in the PTA and other school associations, we become aware of the big picture. In this higher-level capacity, we can influence school policies and determine where the money is best spent.

Unfortunately, as school volunteers, we sometimes encounter pitfalls. Consider these tips:

- ✔ Avoid getting "Trapped in the Loop." Once people know your face and know you and know you can get a job done, a funny thing starts to happen. People heading up committees automatically dial your number whenever a new job comes up. Why? It's more convenient to call someone they already know will come through than to search for new recruits. Pretty soon, though, the same few people are doing all the work. They're not happy about it and neither are the people who feel excluded from the school's "in group." The solution? Just say no. Tell them politely, "I'm already overcommitted. I'm afraid I'll have to pass this one up." Then suggest possible recruits. In chapter 13, we will discuss assertiveness in depth.

✔ Be careful not to overstep your position as a school helper. You are there to help teachers, not to undercut them. Teachers understandably dislike anyone stepping on their professional toes.

✔ Don't expect special privileges for your child in return for your work.

✔ If you find yourself in a position of leadership, take care of your volunteers. Don't exploit the good workers.

Choosing an Organization That's Right for You

Choosing a school or church where you want to donate your time is easy. However, picking the right charitable institution or non-profit organization can be overwhelming. Usually volunteers base their decision on either or both of two factors mentioned earlier: (1) personal interest or (2) the opportunity to work in areas in which they already have training or will be trained to do. For example, a personal experience may lead a volunteer to choose Mothers Against Drunk Driving or the American Cancer Society. Or a passionate love of art history may lead a volunteer to train as an art docent.

Volunteer jobs are not limited to charities. All sorts of non-profit organizations dealing with the arts, conservation, politics, the environment, housing, better government— everything under the sun—need good workers.

Thoroughly investigate the organization you're thinking about joining. Talk to people who volunteer there to find out exactly what they do, whether there are training opportunities, and when and where the meetings are. If new members start out stuffing envelopes, how long does it usually take to move on to something more challenging. How much hands-on work is there with the people you're helping? What about daycare?

Are there hidden costs? What are the perks? For example, after a person volunteers a certain number of hours as a docent at the Stanford University Museum of Art, she is entitled to audit art courses at the university.

Make sure to consider Luks' four factors in order to maximize the benefits from helping. How much time will you actually be spending with the people you're helping? Remember the "sharing the ideals" concept. Will you be getting enough of the camaraderie and fellowship you need?

Don't rule out an organization because of assumptions based on old information. The Junior League, for example, has shed its once-genteel image. Junior Leaguers now work on issues such as drug and alcohol abuse, shelters for women, AIDS, and teen pregnancy.

Pace Yourself

Volunteering can be a lifelong activity. There is no need to start off sprinting. The following pointers will keep you from burning up the track and your own enthusiasm before you're even around the first turn.

- ✔ Start with a small commitment and then build up. You'd never expect yourself to go from walking to running a marathon overnight. The same is true for volunteering; it's a gradual building-up process. What is impossible today may be within reach tomorrow.

- ✔ When you begin, it can be difficult to judge the magnitude of the job you've been asked to do. You might not have the experience nor the information. But you can talk to those who can give you the information you need to make an informed decision. Buy time to do this information gathering by saying, "I'll think about it and get back to you."

- ✔ Don't allow yourself to be pressured into taking a job you don't have interest in or don't have time for. You'll be resentful and won't do your best work. Ultimately, working on a job you hate may cause you to quit volunteering altogether.

Build a Future through Volunteer Work

Instead of just doing whatever volunteer work comes along, you can build a base for a future career through carefully selected volunteer jobs. You can get experience in a field you're investigating, and quite often your volunteer job can be a steppingstone into another career. You can make valuable contacts that may develop later into client and customer bases.

Sara, forty, who had stayed at home raising her three children for twelve years, parlayed volunteer work into the part-time paid job of her dreams. Before children, she had worked as a production assistant in the CBS newsroom in New York. Always dreaming of getting back into her field, she was convinced she had been out of the action too long. Then she volunteered to produce a video the school district was planning to use in its campaign to pass a parcel tax. "I did the equivalent of two in-depth courses in video-production," said Sara of the long, frustrating hours she spent writing, shooting, editing, producing, and directing. The parcel tax committee was thrilled with the professional quality of her tape. Six months later, in another civic group, she volunteered to produce a leadership video for the YWCA. This project went more smoothly and the product was even better. By the time she had finished both videos, she had made several valuable contacts in her field. She was still shocked, however, when an independent video producer of a post-production house where she had volunteered tapped her for a paid part-time position as a producer of corporate videos.

Where do you look for a volunteer job that has possibilities for career training? Talk with friends to see what kind of volunteer work they're doing or know abut. Check with people with whom you do business: your banker, veterinarian, insurance agent, accountant, lawyer, doctor, or any friend who is involved in the type of work you enjoy.

Tips for Getting Over the Rough Spots

In the world of volunteering, all is not sweetness and light and the brotherhood of man. Here are some ideas to get you over the inevitable rough spots that are a part of any job.

- ✔ If you don't enjoy a particular volunteer job, don't assume volunteer work per se is the problem. Try something different. There's no shame in giving up on a particular effort when you are in a situation that isn't right for you.

- ✔ Don't expect to save the world. Sister Teresa hasn't been able to eliminate human suffering and neither will you. Focus on and enjoy the small successes you have in the process of helping, not on the end result.

- ✔ Adopt a Zen-like attitude of "When you sit, sit. When you stand, stand." Translation? When you're doing your volunteer work, concentrate on the task at hand. Concentrate especially on the people you're helping. Clear your mind of anxiety-producing thoughts about the laundry piling up at home or about how much you would be earning if you were being paid for this.

- ✔ Realize that it's normal to experience lows. Even volunteer work you love is bound to have some drudgery attached. Projects don't always go well. After all, volunteer work is just that: work. By definition then, we all would probably rather be playing a game of tennis or leisurely reading the paper.

- ✔ Avoid burnout. When you have worked too hard for too long, you may feel overworked, unappreciated, and underloved. You may believe you are neglecting your family in order to get everything done. Volunteering should never be at your family's expense. Keeping a balance between your homelife and your work in the community is important. If you start to feel burnt out, vow to ramp down your commitments as soon as possible. In the meantime, delegate part of your job, even if you're not confident the person you're asking can do it well. And most importantly, learn to "Just Say No." This is the time to seek out the company and comfort of good friends. Discuss your burnout with them and see if they can help you figure out creative ways to relieve your burden.

✔ Finally, spend some peaceful time alone so that you can "fill up" after so much giving of your skills and love. Reflect on these words, which contain the essential spirit of the volunteer work that has temporarily drained your energy:

I expect to pass through life but once. If therefore, there be any kindness I can show or any good I can do to any fellow being, let me do it now, and not defer or neglect it, as I shall not pass this way again.

— William Penn[2]

Exercises for Developing Your Volunteer Mission

1. Assess your current status as a volunteer. Ask yourself the following questions:

---

[2] As quoted in Laurence J. Peter, *Peter's Quotations* (New York: William Morrow & Co., 1977), 279.

a. Where and how often do you volunteer?

b. Which of these jobs do you enjoy the most? Why?

c. Would you like to drop any of these volunteer activities? If so, why? Analyze these jobs in terms of your own interests and opportunities for training.

d. Do you enjoy the people you work with?

e. Do you work with other volunteers as much as you would like?

f. Do you ever experience "helper's high?" Describe when and why.

g. What would have to happen for your volunteer work to become more satisfying? Name three positive changes.

h. How are your recruiting skills? What women have you recruited for volunteer work in recent years? Can you think of three women who might be interested? Think in particular about women who are new to the area. Remember that the reason why many women don't volunteer is that they've never been asked.

2. Assess your current training/skills by working through the following questions:

a. In what areas have you received useful training in volunteer work?

b. Are there any jobs in which you could directly apply these skills? Name three that interest you.

c. Name three areas in which you would like training.

d. For what paid jobs would this training prepare you?

e. Name three organizations in which you could receive this training.

f. What phone calls do you need to make to gather more information about finding opportunities to get the training you want and finding a job using these skills.

Part Two

Business Matters

6

Homing In on Housework

In my mother's day, homemaking wasn't looked down
on. I want to make homemaking glamorous again.
— Martha Stewart[1]

Homemaker extraordinaire Martha Stewart publishes
the upscale and updated women's magazine, *Martha Stewart
Living*. In it she teaches us how to sew organdy dresses for our
daughters, create regulation badminton courts for family gatherings, and hunt Easter eggs in topiary gardens. Her idea of a
"quickie" meal? Galette of root vegetables and vanilla ice
cream with rhubarb-blackberry compote.

In her magazine she portrays a fantasy world of home that
is far away from the realities of small children, houses that need
cleaning and fixing up, and bounced checks. But the fabulous
Ms. Stewart and the more prosaic practitioners of the domestic
arts like myself do have something in common. Among other
things, we both recognize the importance of homemaking.
Martha Stewart glamorizes and glorifies domesticity; we

---

[1] As quoted by Cynthia Crossen, "*Martha Stewart Living*: Fantasies for 3,"
Wall Street Journal (March 28, 1991): B1.

merely pay our respects. Yet both attitudes reflect a desire for a clean and ordered home. From there family members can go forth refreshed and organized and better able to cope with the challenges of daily life.

Plain or fancy, what matters is that our homes provide the comfort and warmth we all need. For many of us, the simple pleasures of fresh sheets, clean clothes, polished wood and an occasional bouquet of flowers on the table suffice.

Now for the bad news: Plain or fancy, what keeps the comfort and warmth flowing at home and hearth is usually one woman doing a multitude of household tasks. While the more creative and satisfying aspects of homemaking—decorating, crafts, sewing, cooking and entertaining—take time and concentration, the distinctly unglamorous laundry, dishwashing, and cleaning are just plain monotonous. Yet, the sad fact is, no home can function without the drudgery detail.

All at-home mothers face the same dilemma: How can we possibly do the work necessary for the kind of home we've always dreamed of when small children are right behind undoing what we've just done? How can we keep from letting housework consume all our free time?

What follows are ideas to help you maintain your home the way you want without dusting yourself and your own dreams into a corner in the process.

As we discussed in chapter 2, the broad choices regarding housework are:

1. Do it all and take pride in it.

2. Do the minimum and forget the rest.

3. Negotiate with your husband or other family members to share household responsibilities.

4. Hire it out.

Don't gloss over the third option. At the very least, everybody in the house should pitch in on a regular basis, not just for emergencies. You can negotiate some jobs with your spouse. If you hate to go to discount food stores and he hates to prune bushes, maybe you can work a trade. Once you've worked out this general decision, you can apply the following guidelines to whatever housework remains.

We will first look at ways to set realistic standards for housework, which will free you from thinking that your housework is "never done." Then we will design a flexible schedule to make housework more manageable and, perhaps, enjoyable.

Organizing Your Housework

Step One: Downsize Your Workload

Look over your housework tasks carefully and decide what you're not going to do.

Journalist Quentin Crisp wrote: "There was no need to do any housework at all. After the first four years, the dirt doesn't get any worse." We can use the half-truth in that statement to trim down our workloads. When the dust particles on newly cleaned mini-blinds and woodwork reappear within a few days, we are justifiably dismayed. However, once the dust reaches "critical mass," its build-up seems to level off. I've noticed the same pattern with cobwebs on ceiling fixtures, dustballs in closets, and socks and pencils behind the dryer. This leveling-off phenomenon plus the fact that this sort of dirt is mostly invisible provide two good reasons to eliminate these chores from your list of regular household tasks. Round up dustbunnies once a year and call it good. If nobody will notice it, don't do it, or at least don't do it often.

Step Two: Set Your Own Standards

Free yourself from inherited notions of the "right" way to run a home, especially if they don't make sense for you. You don't have to wash lettuce and vegetables before putting them in the refrigerator. You don't have to line the shelves in the pantry. You don't have to spring clean.

Every April my mother religiously attacks enemy dirt in her house like Napoleon at Austerlitz. She moves every stick of furniture, ferrets out dirt lurking underneath chairs and in unlikely corners, rips down curtains and overturns mattresses. In the springtime I prefer to enjoy the new flowers and fresh breezes. My curtains stay on their hooks until they look soiled; my mattresses reside permanently on their box springs. In the fall, however, when the older girls are back in school and the weather is less inviting, I do a modified blitz of deep cleaning. I live with the fact that my house will never be as ship-shape as the home I grew up in. If well-meaning relatives or friends criticize my blasphemous attitude toward certain household tasks they hold sacred, I invite them over to help me with the work.

Step Three: Make a List of Household Tasks That You Want to Do

Think carefully about the tasks you do routinely or those that you intend to do but never seem to get around to doing. Are they all important to you? I love clean windows and mirrors, the look of just-vacuumed carpets, and a good evening meal. I couldn't care less about how neatly my pots and pans are organized or how shiny the inside of my oven looks. Put the tasks that aren't important to you on the backburner and do them only occasionally.

Consult your family as you reset priorities. If your husband loves a well-organized refrigerator and a crumb-free kitchen floor, consider putting those items at the top of your list—or at the top of his. If your children tell you they love the summer vegetable garden and the dollhouse in the family room, don't eliminate the maintenance of these items.

Make a list of weekly jobs. These might include such items as laundry, ironing, watering plants, mopping floors, vacuuming, grocery shopping, changing beds, etc. Then make a list of monthly jobs such as cleaning the refrigerator or oven and mending. Finish up with quarterly tasks—straightening drawers, vacuuming sofas and chairs—and annual events—cleaning out the basement or garage, shampooing the carpets and washing walls.

Step Four: Design a Cleaning Schedule

To begin, choose one of the two basic cleaning schedules:

1. the traditional "Friday is cleaning day" approach, in which you devote a whole day exclusively to housework, or

2. the flexible schedule, in which you do a portion of your housework every day.

If you have small children, I advocate the flexible schedule. First, one day with little ones underfoot never has enough hours in it. Second, because the house will never get completely out of shape the way it does with the everything-on-one-day approach, special circumstances won't throw you. You can easily adjust a flexible schedule by catching up on the must-do's the next day. Let the other things ride until the same day next week rolls around.

Take the list of household tasks that you have just completed and assign the tasks to days of the week based on your scheduled activities and personal preferences. Keep these guidelines in mind as you design your plan:

✔ Schedule according to your cleaning method. Do you clean room-by-room or task-by-task? For example, if you're a room-by-roomer, you might schedule the living room and dining room for Monday; if you're a task-by-tasker, you might schedule dusting the whole house and cleaning mirrors for Monday.

✔ Try to schedule around your other activities in a logical way. For example, if you usually do marketing on Thursdays, perhaps Thursday morning or Wednesday would be a good day to clean the refrigerator. If playgroup comes to

your house on Thursdays, clean the family
room on Friday, and so on.

✔ Build "project days" into your schedule. On
those weeks when you want to clean out closets
or cupboards, organize a workroom, or plant
spring bulbs, plan to let your other things go as
much as possible. Never fear, the task will roll
around again next week.

✔ Set a limit on the amount of time you spend on
housework every day. I like to finish most of
my housework by midmorning; later in the
afternoon, I do "follow-up work" and cook
dinner. Tell yourself that if you're still not done
by lunchtime or your baby's naptime, you will
call it quits.

✔ Rethink your schedule as needs change. For
example, as babies move into the toilet training
phase, you may need to concentrate more time
on sanitizing the bathroom while you devote
less time to diaper duty.

Step Five: Declutter Your House in Ten-Minute Increments

Do you have things stacked up in cupboards or corners
because there is no place to put them? Do you sometimes
"lose" things in your house? With just ten minutes a day, three
trash bags, and some dedication to the cause, your house can
go from pigpen to paradise. Interested? Here's what you need
to do:

✔ Decide which area of clutter bugs you the most.
Set aside ten minutes (I made it ten because
sometimes that's the maximum an at-home
mother of small children can get) to attack the
mess. Plan to work like crazy for ten minutes,
then go back to what you were doing before.

✔ Take three trash bags and label them "Throw," "Give," and "Put Away." The "Throw" bag will go to the trash; the "Give" bag will go to charity or friends; the contents of the "Put Away" bag (items you want to save) go to into boxes which you will label.

✔ Post yourself and your three bags in front of the area you want to declutter. Remove everything from the area. Your job now is to make a decision for every item you pulled out: If it doesn't belong in the area, put it in one of the three bags.

Let's say you want to clean out your "killer closet," so named because a deadly cascade of gloves without mates, tennis balls, a throw-rug you hate, and a bag of clothes for charity tumbles on your head if you try to remove even the smallest item. After removing everything, put back in the storage area only those things which belong in there. Make a pile of items which belong somewhere else and—this is important—put them where they belong *right now!* Stray Legos go straight to the Lego set, not to another clutter area to be put away later. And no, you will probably never have those broken umbrellas fixed. If in doubt, throw it out! Don't be lazy! Keep going. Bag it now!

Tips for Making Housework a Positive Experience

Now that you've organized a plan for your housework, here are some things to think about that will help you keep that positive energy flowing as you actually do the work.

Establish House Rules

Now that your house is de-cluttered, keep it that way by establishing some "house rules." Here are some possibilities:

✔ **Don't put it down; put it away.** Discipline yourself and others in your family to deal with an item immediately. Put it in its proper place then and there. Do not stick it in a soon-to-be-cluttered-again corner to put away later. If you live in a two-story home, put a basket at the foot of the stairs to fill with items that need to be put away upstairs. This brings us to our second house rule:

✔ **Never go upstairs empty-handed.** Always carry laundry or the myriad items in a household that always need to be put away.

✔ **Clean as you go.** This principle is important especially in kitchen work. In this way you avoid having to eat a meal surrounded by an assortment of dirty pans and empty cans. My mother always tried to impress me with the importance of this one, but it wasn't until I had my own children that I realized how trashed out a kitchen or bathroom can get in a short amount of time if this rule isn't followed.

✔ **If you made the mess, you clean up the mess.** This is especially important for children to learn. Mom is not everyone's clean-up crew. Naturally, this applies only to those family members who are old enough to actually carry out this responsibility. Furthermore, there are some messes involving glass or grape juice or cleaning chemicals you will always want to do yourself.

✔ When in doubt, throw it out. This rule will keep you from having to go through the marathon form of the three-bag drill ever again!

Involve Your Kids in Housework

Although small children may seem to be the natural enemies of housework, letting them help can actually be fun for all parties. You can put your baby in a Snuggli or backpack; babies love to watch the activity and will be entertained by your words if you talk about what you're doing.

Housework with toddlers is like playing a game of "house" with real equipment. Naturally exuberant and "helpful," they love to dust, wash plastic dishes, wind up the vacuum cord, fold washcloths, match socks, and deliver laundry to rooms. Make sure you stop frequently to admire your work and if your children are helping you, theirs. Stand back and take a long look at a beautiful stack of laundered towels, a clean window, a pretty table setting. In this way you remind yourself of and you teach children early on an important lesson in life: appreciation for a job well done. Many self-critical adults have never fully mastered this lesson.

Assign older children regular chores. Emptying waste baskets, sorting and folding laundry, clearing and loading dishes into the dishwasher, and stripping and making beds are all ways older children can make important contributions to the household. Working alone is drudgery for people of all ages. But working together is a great opportunity to catch up on the news as well as the chores. For example, if I'm cooking dinner, Maggie's unloading the dishwasher, Anne's folding laundry on the kitchen table, and little Elizabeth is "washing" the dishes at the sink, this gives us a chance to share our days and laugh together. We strengthen our relationships as we share the daily rituals.

Don't let jobs become gender-specific. Little boys can wash dishes and Windex counter-tops as well as little girls. The next generation of wives will thank you for this early training!

Likewise, little girls can carry out the trash and tidy up the backyard.

Make One Room Off-Limits to Kids

Knowing that just one room is clutter-free can provide you with a great psychological boost. It soothes the soul just to gaze upon a neat and tidy living area. Furthermore, if a friend drops by unannounced, you know there will be a peaceful retreat where you can enjoy each other's adult company.

Think Twice Before You Buy New Household Goods

Appliances that supposedly save work—food processors, bread machines and even the lowly garlic press—don't always save time. At the very least they must all be cleaned and stored after use. And one new acquisition tends to generate others. For example, a shiny new espresso machine seems an innocent enough purchase. But you will also need to buy and maintain a coffee grinder, which in turn means you must shop for fine coffee beans and, to really "do it right," special espresso cups and saucers and other standard espresso accouterments. Doesn't it sound simpler and more fun just to drive to the local coffee house where trained professionals serve us a perfect latte or cappuccino in a perfect cup with a perfect cinnamon topping?

Polish Up Your Sense of Humor

A sense of humor is the best defense against taking housework too seriously. Like any other skill, humor can be cultivated. Consider the following to strengthen your "hausfrau humor."

- ✔ Collect in a "humor file" funny cartoons and jokes that feature housework.

- ✔ Read a copy of *Martha Stewart Living* just to revel in all the things you're not doing.

✔ Read Erma Bombeck's column or her books. With her sarcastic but affectionate descriptions of housework, Bombeck has comforted generations of homemakers with the knowledge that someone else knows what we're going through. Bombeck once described how her mother had always been disappointed in her lack of interest in domesticity. Once, when a small envelope fell out of her daughter's pantry, Bombeck's mother picked it up and gasped, "Oh, my soul. Do you have any idea of the expiration date on this packet of yeast? It expired July 28, 1957. What happened?" "I don't like to be pressured by a deadline," Bombeck replied.

Turn On Music to Clean By

No doubt about it, housework is a physical workout. Take your cue from exercise instructors, who find that music promotes higher energy levels. Who could possibly stop scrubbing with the Pointer Sisters' "Neutron Dance," a Sousa march, or anything upbeat playing in the background?

Make Your Priorities "People First, House Second"

At-home mothers are trying to get away from the word "housewife" because it implies that we are married to a collection of wood, brick and shingles. The concept of putting our relationship with this house and the objects in it above the people in our lives seems ridiculous. We try to hold the attitude that the dust will always be there; the people won't.

But sometimes women lose the "people first, house second" frame of mind and fall into the pitfall of "compulsive housekeeping." To compulsive housekeepers, people are a threat. Everything becomes a "Don't": Don't track in on my floors! Don't sit down there...or there! Don't eat; you'll leave crumbs! Don't touch the counter, the walls, the door knobs, the walls...or anything!

The real tragedy of compulsive housekeeping is that a woman forfeits important, life-sustaining relationships by making her house her top priority. While she may be trying to prove her worth by applying herself tirelessly to her home, in reality she sends out another message: the furniture and carpets are more important than her family and friends. Keeping up the house, she keeps up with nothing else.

"Just Do It"

Contrary to popular thought, motivation does not necessarily precede action. In fact, the opposite is often true. The act of doing something primes the pump of motivation. Just start cleaning the bathroom or re-organizing your closet. Soon you'll be involved (or motivated) in the activity. If you wait until you're in the mood, you may wait forever.

Reward Yourself. No One Else Will!

Unabated housework can be a brutalizing experience. After an hour of shuttling back and forth from one corner of the house to the other, handling and breathing in toxic cleaning sprays and powders, take a break. Fix a cup of tea and go outside for some fresh air. Phone a friend and make some fun aprés-cleaning plans.

Think of perks you can give yourself after completing a particularly odious task. Say to yourself, "After I've finished cleaning the shower, I will put the baby down for a nap and I will enjoy a leisurely lunch. Then I will curl up for an hour with my favorite magazine." Or treat yourself to a luxurious bubble bath and a manicure in the evening while your husband reads to the kids.

The Simpler, the Better

Reflect on this Amish philosophy of housework to gain inner peace as you work. In Sue Bender's delightful evocation of life among the Amish, *Plain and Simple*, she describes a domesticity that stands in refreshing contrast to that of Martha

Stewart, with whom I began this chapter. The Amish eschew anything at all glamorous; for them, the plainer and simpler, the better. Accordingly, the Amish revere the "daily practices that give life its stability and framework"—what we call housework. Everything is a ritual. The steps for how best to wash, dry and put away cups have already been determined and are carefully taught to succeeding generations. Whereas so many of us rush madly through our chores so that we can get on to the things we want to do, the Amish feel no need to hurry. Relaxed and free, they actually enjoy the process itself—not just the end result—of performing their "chores of silent grace."

Exercises for Developing Your Housework Mission

1. Which of the following statements best describes your housework situation?

    ☐ I do all of it and take pride in it.

    ☐ I do all of it and resent it.

    ☐ I do the minimum and leave the rest.

    ☐ I do the minimum but that's still too much.

    ☐ I delegate or hire much of it out.

2. Are you satisfied with your housework situation? Why or why not?

3. What three things about housework do you dislike the most?

4. What three aspects of housework do you like the most?

5. What "products" of housework—clean windows, clean clothes, hot food, etc.—are most important to you? To your husband? To your children?

6. What household jobs do your spouse and children prefer to do?

7. What are your standards for housework?

☐ Very high. My home is immaculate.

☐ Fairly high. My home is usually clean and straightened.

☐ Average. My home is messy but basically clean.

☐ Below average. My home is quite messy and needs cleaning.

☐ Low. My home is a filthy mess.

8. Are you satisfied with your standards? How did you arrive at these standards (you and your husband decided; it's the way your mother did it; it's the most you can possibly do)?

9. Do you do as much housework as your mother did? Does that concern you? Do you do different household tasks than your mother did? Have you eliminated any tasks that your mother did?

10. How much time do you spend every day doing "hands-on" housework?

11. Are there any household tasks that are not important or necessary to you, which you could eliminate?

12. What three jobs could you delegate to older children? To your husband? Could you hire out smaller jobs such as dress shirt ironing?

13. List three tasks that you could eliminate or find alternative ways of accomplishing.

14. Make a list of all the household tasks that remain. Include big projects you do regularly and one-time-only projects you anticipate.

15. Design a weekly schedule using either the all-on-one-day or the flexible schedule. In parentheses, write in other activities you do that day (grocery shopping, manicure, ballet lessons) and chores that older children do that may impact your housework schedule.

16. Write down three things you could use as perks after heavy housework.

7

Earning by Saving

For Yolanda Achanzar, going to work was like listening
to an old-fashioned cash register ring....She'd drop off
her two toddlers with a sitter (ka-ching: $29 a day).
She'd commute to the office in her Mercury Villager
(ka-ching: $8). She'd dig into her purse for breakfast and
lunch (ka-ching: $10). And she'd dress up for work
(ka-ching: $5 a day, $8.50 if she snagged her hose, $12.50
if you include the dry-cleaning bills)....

— Mark Schwannhauser

Many of us can add up those work-related ka-chings
we've eliminated by coming home. Add to that the tidy sum
we save by shrewd financial planning (a.k.a. sticking to a
budget) and we can come up with whopping annual savings.
Does at-home motherhood pay? It does if we look at saving
money as earning money. It does if, instead of earning a
paycheck, we use our time as an edge to rip and cut away at
high prices and needless spending.

Those of us who have quit our jobs can start with the
bonus our families will realize by eliminating hidden work
expenses. Taxes will be the biggest (and most often over-

looked) chunk of cash savings. (You don't pay taxes on income you don't earn, and often a second salary pushes a family income into a higher tax bracket.) Add to that amount the state and Social Security taxes we won't be paying out. Next add the high cost of childcare, which goes up with each child.

Other hidden savings include what we will no longer be spending on our dress-for-success wardrobe and dry-cleaning bills, transportation costs (gas, maintenance, parking), restaurant food (breakfasts and lunches out, frozen dinners, and meals out when we and our spouses are too exhausted to cook), and housecleaning and minor repair costs, which are no longer necessary with us at home.

Something Has to Give

Those of us who have quit work can look forward to all these immediate savings, but our families will still have to manage on a smaller income. Consider this challenge to be a growth experience (with emphasis on growing pains!). Adjusting to a smaller income boils down to one thing: a belt-tightening budget.

The specifics will vary from family to family. For some, staying at home may mean staying in a smaller home in a less prestigious neighborhood or even deferring indefinitely the dream of owning a home. For others, it may mean selling a second home and giving up weekend trips to the wine country and expensive dinners in French restaurants. We learn to turn off lights, to buy clothes at discount stores, to cut our children's hair. We repair our aging car a few more times instead of buying a new one. In themselves, some of these measures are small potatoes, but they add up to make a big difference at the end of each month.

Hammering out and (here comes the painful part) holding to a tighter budget involves foregoing some of the material goods and services that many of us "material girls in a material world" have come to believe we are entitled to. Making the necessary sacrifices to reduce spending is not easy when all around us people—especially our dual-income friends—seem to be doing and purchasing expensive, exciting things.

For many of us, this will be the first time we have had to be resourceful. For the first time, we develop a thoughtful and questioning approach to spending money. We learn to ask ourselves, "Do we really need this, or do we merely want it?"

Make no mistake. Managing your finances so that you can earn by saving means extra work. Living on less demands patience, flexibility, creativity, and high-level problem-solving skills—and lots of time. But remember, for many of us, it was even more work to spend eight hours away from home to earn dollars that were often needlessly spent.

Look at it this way. Let's say you spend an average of one hour a day exploiting savings opportunities. Most financial planners agree that we can trim our budgets ten percent without even feeling it; much more is possible if we're willing to work harder. Add that number to the hidden costs of working. Not a bad return for your time investment at home.

And here's the kicker: It is more profitable to save one dollar (what we're doing now) than to add one dollar of income (what some of us were doing at our jobs). Why? Because in order to earn at a job one real dollar of spendable income, you have to earn a dollar plus the tax portion. Let's say you were in the twenty percent tax bracket. You would have to earn $1.20 in order to have one real dollar to spend. When you reduce your spending by a dollar (or save it), you earn the equivalent of $1.20!

Lest you start feeling deprived, keep one fundamental point in mind: Everybody—including the affluent—needs to control spending. Furthermore, no matter how rich you are, no income will ever be large enough to buy everything you want. Budgets, by helping you prioritize, enable you to control wasteful spending so that you will have money for the things you really want. True luxuries will probably need to be postponed. Your goal should be to *tame* the spending beast; there is no need to savagely squeeze the life out of it and every dollar that comes your way.

Do You Need a Budget?

Not everybody needs a formal budget, of course. Some of us seem to be blessed with a natural ability to live within our incomes. Mark "T" for "True" and "F" for "False" in response to the following questions, which will help you determine if this is true for you:

_____ We find it necessary to regularly use money from savings to pay monthly expenses.

_____ We find it impossible to maintain a regular savings program.

_____ We often charge everyday expenses and are unable to pay in full at the end of the month.

_____ One or the other of us hides certain purchases from the other because we're embarrassed about how much they cost.

_____ We overdraw our bank account regularly.

_____ We avoid discussing financial matters since we usually end up having a fight.

_____ In the past six months, we've received overdue notices from creditors.

_____ We're always shocked at the large amount due on our credit card bills.

_____ We have had to borrow money to pay off our bills.

If your response was "True" to one or more of these statements, you can benefit from a simple, flexible outline to help you develop better spending habits. In short, you need a budget.

A budget helps because it forces you to make conscious decisions about where your money goes each month. Couples who go from two incomes to one, vaguely thinking, "Oh, we'll just cut back a little; things will work out," are usually doomed to frantic anxiety at the end of every month. Although a budget can't guarantee financial success, the lack of one practically guarantees problems.

How to Make a Budget

Use the budget sheets on pages 95-96 to simplify the process for you. Work in pencil so that you can erase and amend figures as you and your husband work through the four-step process.

1. In the "Income" workspace, fill in what you bring in each month. In the "Expenses" workspace, write down what you think you spend in all categories. Include everything. Refer to your checkbook, credit card bills, and receipts to insure accurate information. For a month, you and your husband should carry a little notebook in which you write down every seemingly inconsequential expenditure—$1.50 for a large Coke, $1.25 at the copy machine, everything! Divide the costs of annual expenses such as summer camp or insurance premiums by twelve. Now total the items. Subtract your total monthly expenses from your total monthly income. If you come up with a surplus, congratulations and keep doing what you're doing; "if it ain't broke, don't fix it." But if your answer pops up in red ink, that means you're broke and you need to fix it, so keep going.

2. If you're spending too much, you will need to take out your budgeting knife and trim off some of the fat. One way to approach the task is to label all categories in your budget either

"Necessity" or "Want." After you've done that, go through the necessities item-by-item to see if there is a cheaper way to obtain the same thing. For example, your mortgage is clearly a necessity. But when interest rates are low, perhaps you could refinance your mortgage. This would result in lower monthly payments. Now fix your beady eyes on your wants to see what, if any, of these you can postpone, cut out, or replace with something cheaper. For example, every week the fashion section of our local newspaper features a column with photographs of two models in almost identical outfits: one is wearing a designer outfit and accessories; the other a budget version of the same look. Often the difference in price is $500 or more. This same principle of achieving the look of quality by careful shopping can be applied to many areas of discretionary spending.

3. Before you write down a final figure, you and your husband have a lot of talking to do. Discuss your income and budget as a husband-and-wife team. Warning: Individual differences in spending habits and money management may rear their ugly heads during this process and cause conflicts. With less money to work with, you and your husband may disagree about how the scarcer funds should be spent. You may think babysitters during the day and lunches out are a necessity; he may think that's nice if you can afford it, but you can't. You may want to save the Christmas bonus; he may want to splurge on a new stereo system.

You must negotiate your differences. The big spender might agree to halt all big purchases until you build up a three-month emergency fund. Then the spender can splurge on the stereo, within limits you both agree upon. In this way, no one partner has to give up what he or she thinks is vital.

4. Vow to each other and to yourselves that you will follow through on the cuts you've decided upon. A budget is more than an exercise in pencil-pushing. Simple records will help you stay on track. Make twelve copies of the budget form; every month tally up what you actually spent and enter the numbers in the correct space. Then compare these to the budget you've decided upon and plan to make the necessary adjustments to reconcile the differences. For example, if you overspend in the clothing category by $100, plan to cut back by the same amount the following month so that your budget will balance. By tracking what you actually spend, you can see if your estimate was accurate or not and revise if necessary. Be willing to re-evaluate priorities. You may see too much money going for entertainment and clothing while the family complains that the VCR is shot or the couch is hanging in threads. A family conference may be necessary to re-establish what is essential and what is a luxury.

Our Family Budget — Income

Monthly Net Wages   _____

Interest/Dividends   _____

Bonuses/Tax Refunds   _____

Child Support   _____

Other   _____

Total Monthly Income   _____

Less Monthly Expenses
(from next page)   - _____

Monthly Profit/Loss   = _____

Our Family Budget — Expenses

Shelter	Rent or Mortgage	_____
	Homeowner's/Renter's Insurance	_____
	Maintenance/Improvement	_____
	Owner's Association Fees	_____
	Electricity/Gas	_____
	Telephone	_____
	Water/Sewer	_____
	Garbage	_____
	Household Furnishings	_____
	Other	_____
Food	Groceries	_____
	Meals/Snacks Out	_____
	Other	_____
Adults' Needs	Clothing	_____
	Toiletries/Hair Care	_____
	Other	_____
Children's Needs	Clothing	_____
	Babysitters	_____
	Summer School/Camp	_____
	Tuition	_____
	Tutoring/Lessons	_____
	Sports Fees	_____
	Other	_____
Transportation	Car Payment	_____
	Auto Insurance	_____
	Gas	_____
	Parking/Public Transport	_____
	Maintenance/Repair	_____
	Other	_____
Medical	Health/Disability Insurance	_____
	Uncovered Medical/Pharmacy	_____
	Other	_____
Loans	Credit-Card Payments	_____
	Other	_____
Miscellaneous	Child Support/Alimony	_____
	Savings	_____
	Investments	_____
	Gifts	_____
	Holiday Gifts	_____
	Charities	_____
	Entertainment	_____
	Vacations	_____
	Hobbies	_____
	Magazines/Books/Supplies	_____
	Membership Dues	_____
	Other	_____
	Total Monthly Expenses	_____

Many resources are available to help you with specific ways to save money in all budget categories. *Sylvia Porter's Money Book* and Mary Ann Cahill's *The Heart Has Its Own Reasons* are particularly helpful. Go to your local library and check either of them out. Here are a few ideas I've gleaned from my reading:

Housing

✔ Take advantage of low mortgage rates by refinancing your home. It's probably worth it if your rate drops two percentage points lower than your current rate.

Food

✔ Grow your own veggies and fruit if possible; buy in bulk the items your family likes; and when good deals come along, stockpile staples like mad. See the next chapter for shopping tips.

✔ Plan your meals a week ahead. If you know that chicken tacos will be on the menu two days after you have roast chicken, you will be less likely to waste.

✔ Always use a grocery list—you'll save ten percent by avoiding impulse buying. If possible, shop without children and husbands. Never shop on an empty stomach.

✔ One night a week have a leftover night to avoid waste.

✔ Make several times the normal servings, freeze, and reheat later. These frozen dinners are much less expensive and tastier than buying ready-made frozen foods.

Clothing

- ✔ If you don't plan to sew your clothes, shop the sales with a carefully drawn-up list of items you need. Buy only items on your list, no matter how great a deal you find. See chapter 7 for more clothes shopping tips.

- ✔ Use a brush to remove stains and air woolens to keep fresh.

- ✔ Wash clothes in cold water as much as possible. This prevents fading and wrinkling and prolongs the life of the garment.

Transportation

- ✔ Use public transportation if it is cost- and time-efficient for you.

- ✔ Consider selling one car if your location permits. You can drive your husband to and from work or drive the car on alternate days. You can save a bundle in auto insurance, repairs and maintenance, fees, and gasoline.

- ✔ Be gentle with your big hunk of steel. When you see a stop sign ahead, slow down gently and steadily instead of lurching to a last-minute stop. This type of jack-rabbit driving sucks gas and is hard on brakes.

- ✔ Combine errands as much as possible to save gas.

- ✔ Pump your own gas and do as many minor maintenance tasks and repairs yourself.

- ✔ Have tune-ups at recommended intervals. They save money on fuel and on engine wear; with the high cost of gasoline, regular tune-ups pay for themselves.

✔ Invest in the maintenance manual for your car; both you and your husband can learn to do many of the regular upkeep tasks and repairs yourselves.

✔ Turn off the engine when you're waiting in the school parking lot. It uses more gas to idle for a minute than it does to restart.

Utilities

✔ Contact your utility company for specific information on ways to save energy. Special programs are available to help you use energy more wisely, efficiently and cheaply. For example, our local electric company offers reduced rates if customers sign up for a program in which they do not use major appliances between the peak hours of 1 and 6 P.M.

✔ Slash telephone bills by making it a house rule never to call long-distance during primetime. Check with your local service company for discount times. Start to write postcards or letters.

✔ A refrigerator door hanging open while you're contemplating means the fridge has to work harder to keep things cool. When you're preparing a meal, take everything out of the freezer and refrigerator at one time. Always wait until a dish has cooled before storing so that the fridge doesn't waste energy cooling down a hot dish.

✔ Maintain your refrigerator: vacuum or dust the cooling coils; replace worn out door gaskets; defrost the freezer regularly if needed.

✔ Preheat the oven for baking cakes or breads only. Otherwise, preheating in unnecessary.

✔ Zap foods in your microwave whenever possible, as microwaving uses the same amount of energy in half the time. Use your toaster oven and other small kitchen appliances whenever possible; they use much less energy.

✔ Run full loads when using your washer and dryer. Use hot water only for whites and soiled items. Also, clean lint out; a lint-free machine works more efficiently.

✔ If you have an electric dryer, when it breaks, replace it with a gas model. They are much cheaper to operate.

✔ Use your dishwasher once a day and use the energy-saving setting if possible.

✔ Fluorescent lights provide three times the light incandescent lights do for the same amount of electricity. They also last ten times as long.

✔ Dimmer switches lengthen the life of the bulb while reducing electricity use.

✔ "Lights out" when not in use.

Home Maintenance and Repairs

✔ Do maintenance and repair jobs yourself. Caulking around bathtubs, fixing the garbage disposal, unclogging pipes with a snake aren't all that difficult but cost plenty if you hire it out. A multitude of how-to manuals on these topics are available.

✔ Many appliance manufacturers offer hotlines with trained service technicians who can talk you through repairs step-by-step.

- ✔ If you sew, make bedspreads, curtains and other decorative items for the house using sale fabrics and remnants.

- ✔ Learn to paint and wallpaper.

- ✔ Barter your skills. If you know how to wallpaper and your friend down the street sews, she can make curtains for you while you paper her guestroom.

Medical/Dental

- ✔ Practice preventative medicine and dentistry by encouraging a healthy lifestyle. Encourage all family members to exercise regularly, to eat healthy foods and to brush and floss daily.

- ✔ Shop carefully for medical insurance.

Tuition

- ✔ Cooperative pre-schools are much cheaper. When my friend Katherine's son Shawn was in pre-school, she found she could afford the co-op plus Mother's Day Out (which gave her a day on her own) for the same price as a regular pre-school. See if your child's pre-school will accept volunteer time in lieu of fees.

Childcare

- ✔ Join a babysitting club or co-op, or start one yourself. Trade off regularly with friends to get some "free" time off.

Entertainment

- ✔ Start thinking in terms of recreation as entertainment. Bike riding, hiking, tennis, swims at the city pool are all fun, healthy and inexpensive forms of recreational entertainment.

✔ Search out cheaper "thrills" such as museums, matinee movies, drive-in movies, botanical gardens, planetariums, aquariums, free concerts in the park—and of course, everybody loves a parade.

✔ Take advantage of entertainment specials. Some restaurants offer two-for-one dinners; some theaters offer reduced prices on certain nights. High schools or amateur groups offer quality productions of musicals and plays for a fraction of the cost of a professional show.

✔ Instead of dropping $50 at a pricey restaurant, get together with friends for cozy, intimate evenings at home, afternoon barbecues, or family picnics in the park.

✔ Organize a potluck club with several other couples you enjoy. Get together monthly at someone's home. Everybody brings a dish; nobody goes broke.

✔ If you want to have some friends over but you can't afford a whole meal, invite them over for dessert and coffee.

Vacations

✔ Spend a week in a cabin in a national park or, if you've already got the equipment, go camping.

✔ Visit out-of-town friends and family. Later you can reciprocate.

✔ Vacation in the off-season.

✔ When traveling, take advantage of special airfare and hotel packages. Go to a local grocery store for supplies for cold breakfast and lunches so that you only eat out for dinner.

Books and Magazines

✔ Get your "fix" of your favorite magazines or that new bestseller at your local library. If they don't have the book you want, request it from them. They will either acquire it for their collection, or they can likely borrow it from another library for you.

✔ Arrange a magazine and paperback book-sharing club with friends and neighbors.

✔ Buy books inexpensively from your local library volunteer "Book-Go-Round" or from a nearby Goodwill store.

Classic Budget Blunders

The following are adapted from *Sylvia Porter's Money Book*:

✔ Don't make your budget until you have actually tracked all your expenses.

✔ Don't let the budget become a straitjacket. If it becomes impossible to stick to, the whole process will fail.

✔ Don't arbitrarily slash a budget category. Because food and household expenses are so great and are not fixed, most families slash these two categories. But if you cut without consideration, the budget will break down. For example, if your family loves steak and chicken, they will feel deprived on a "rice and beans" budget.

✔ Don't fail to set aside money for emergencies. They're sure to arise.

✔ Don't neglect savings. Treat savings as a necessity. "Pay yourself first" should be your motto. To keep yourself on a savings schedule, think about setting up automatic payroll deductions or monthly transfers from checking to savings accounts. Some families earmark half of all bonus money—gift checks from relatives, work bonuses, or tax refunds—for savings.

✔ Don't try to fit yourself into someone else's budget. Would you prefer to spend $10,000 on a new car or on a Master's Degree at a private university? A new big-screen TV or a big vacation? Each family approaches these choices differently depending on the individual goals and priorities of family members. There is no sense trying to fit into a ready-made financial plan which ignores your own personal wants and desires.

✔ Deep-six the credit cards. Plan to use them only for emergencies and large purchases that you discuss ahead. If you can't pay for something with cash, then you probably shouldn't be buying it. Most experts agree that credit cards are the number one threat to a balanced budget.

The Bottom Line

Getting spending under control is essential if you are to be at peace with yourself and your family. Whether you find the process grim or challenging, whether you want to zealously pursue every savings opportunity or only a few carefully selected ones, you need to rigorously apply yourself to planning a budget, and then commit yourself to sticking with it.

Working shoulder-to-shoulder with your husband as you try to work out an equitable spending plan can bring you and your husband closer. As you assess your current spending habits, figure out where to cut back, and decide together what goals you want to pursue with the surplus, you will be forced to examine your most closely-held values. Deciding together upon the sacrifices you will both make in order to have you at home can lead to a renewed sense of strength and resolve as a couple.

Earning by saving probably won't make you rich, although it has happened. But you will surely become rich in what Christine Davidson calls in her book *Staying Home Instead* the "emotional luxuries." You will become rich in the proud knowledge that you and your husband are foregoing many of the material luxuries—the flashy new car, the newly decorated living room, the European vacation—in order to have you home with the family. You will also be rich in the quiet dignity and sense of independence that comes from taking positive steps toward an impressive achievement increasingly rare in our times: living within your means.

Exercises for Developing Your Financial Planning Mission

1. How many times did you respond "True" in the "Do You Need a Budget" quiz? Do you need a budget?

2. How often do you and your husband discuss financial planning?

3. What cost-cutting measures do you emphasize in your current budget?

4. What are your budget's weak spots?

5. What are some additional ways you could trim more fat from your spending? List at least three.

8

Shopping Smart

It's a discount jungle out there.
> — One mother returning from a day
> of shopping for fall school clothes

In today's complex and ever-changing marketplace, shopping is serious business. From canned food to cars, from footwear to fine furniture, prices vary even from day to day. Mothers-at-home, often the primary "purchasing agents" for thousands of dollars from the family operating budget, need both knowledge and practical know-how to make the most of what's available in the shopping "jungle." The business savvy they apply to shopping can mean thousands of surplus dollars every year on the bottom line of the family books.

You may already be an "advanced" shopper. Even so, by following the shopping strategies in this chapter, you are bound to save even more money. So put on your shopping shoes and browse through some of these cost-cutting ideas. We'll begin with some general shopping strategies; then we'll focus specifically on food and clothing.

Five Winning Shopping Strategies for Saving on Everything!

1. Shop Around

It's foolish to spend two hours and two gallons of gas bombing around town to save a dime on nailpolish or a quarter on a pair of sunglasses. But it is worthwhile to shop around for items you buy regularly such as food, clothing, and toiletries. It's even more worthwhile when you need a big-ticket item such as a washer or dryer.

Before you start shopping, conduct a market survey of stores in your area. Watch the ads. Talk to other at-home moms to find out where they shop. Do some "field work" by spending a day in the car with the kids to check out shopping possibilities. Look for discount food warehouses in your area such as Sam's or Price Club. Locate the discount and bargain stores such as K-Mart, Wal-Mart and Target. Scope out the factory outlets or off-price stores such as Ross or Loehmann's. Are there second-hand or thrift shops where you can buy and sell children's clothing? A farmer's market? A bread or bakery outlet where you can buy day-old bread and baked goods?

2. Time Your Shopping

Stock up on things you need when prices are seasonally reduced. You can save thousands just by timing your buying strategically throughout the year. Some seasonal buying opportunities are obvious: Christmas presents in January, bathing suits after the Fourth of July, strawberries in June.

Of course, buy produce when it's in season. But shop the seasonal sales for clothing as well. For example, spring clothes first appear in January. Then in May, when inventories and demand are low, the spring stock's prices are reduced. Three other traditional times for store-wide clearance sales are after Easter, after Fourth of July 4, and after Christmas. You can find additional savings by watching the ads for big sales at the larger department stores: end-of-the-month clearance sales, pre-inventory sales, President's Day sales, and so on. For super savings, wait till what's left from the seasonal sales is reduced!

Other items are traditionally on sale at set times of the year. "White" goods—underwear, lingerie, and sheets, and towels—are on sale in January and August, furniture in August, luggage in July.

If you know there's going to be a sale, shop as early as you can to enjoy the biggest variety in styles, sizes, and colors.

3. Shop for Quality

Don't just shop price; shop quality as well. Sometimes the extra luxury or practicality of higher-priced items is well worth it. That's the beauty of shopping sales: you can buy top quality merchandise with all the extras that you want or need. If you bought at full-price, you might only be able to afford the bottom of the line.

However, don't waste money on quality you don't need. For example, don't overspend for name-brand quality clothes for a child who outgrows her clothes before she wears them out. Similarly, don't pay for high-quality tomatoes to put in soups and stews when slightly bruised ones will taste just as delicious.

Sometimes you need to consider the quality of the store itself, its return policy and the services it provides. A generous return policy is sometimes worth the extra cost. For example, I learned the hard way to purchase Christmas presents for my husband from the finer department stores that have liberal return policies. Too often that "perfect" tie or sweater I selected at a store where "all sales are final" ended up as mothbait in a dark closet corner. Unworn clothes are the biggest waste of all! Of course, even at the finest department stores, I head for the sale rack!

When you are shopping for big-ticket items, buy only from reputable dealers who will stand behind their products.

Recognizing quality can be tricky even for the most astute shopper. Avoid mistakes by doing your homework. Talk to others about brands of food, clothing, and appliance lines to learn which labels they rely upon. Consult consumer magazines at your local library to see what the experts think before you buy.

4. Recognize What Is Not a Bargain

Don't skimp on essentials; it will cost you more in the long run. Cheap hamburger meat with high fat content, winter clothing that's not warm enough, and shoes that pinch your feet are not bargains, regardless of the price. Such "bargains" can turn out to be quite expensive in terms of doctor bills and/or replacement costs.

Furthermore, bulk and economy sizes are only bargains when you will use the entire amount. Otherwise, spoilage and waste will devour your apparent savings. Giant cans of tomato paste are only good buys when you're planning a spaghetti dinner for a large crowd. What's the use of the jumbo carton of plain yogurt if your family only likes the kind with fruit in the bottom?

5. Avoid Impulse Buying

"It's just not worth it to fix up the old one."

""This is a once-in-a-lifetime deal."

"I owe it to myself. Besides, I won't buy any clothes for six months."

"I know we can't afford it, but...."

"I'll do it just this once."

"I've just got to have that."

"The payments won't amount to much because they're spread out."

When tempted to make an impulse buy, give yourself the "time-out treatment." Put the desired item on hold. Then put your money or credit card back in your purse, drive straight home, sit down, take a deep breath, and look around at all the stuff you already have. Ask yourself these questions:

✔ Do I really need this?

✔ Do I already have something similar?

✔ Could I substitute something cheaper for this item?

✔ Is the price reasonable?

✔ Is this the best time to buy the item?

✔ Will it truly satisfy an inner need?

✔ Can I afford it?

If, after taking this self-test, you still think you would be making a wise purchase, go for it.

How to Slash Your Food Costs

If you and your husband were a childless, dual-income couple, you could get away with stopping off at the market after work to pick up dinner. But with a growing family to feed, this casual approach carries too big a pricetag. The following guidelines and tips will help you develop a system for food shopping that will help you slash away at the ever-rising cost of food, often the second biggest, if not the biggest category in the family budget.

Stockpile Like Mad

As I said in chapter 7, your basic strategy should be to grow your own if possible, buy in bulk the items your family likes, and stockpile like mad. Even if you don't have your own land, don't give up on the gardening idea. Check to see if your city sponsors community gardens. The city provides the land; you provide the seeds and sweat.

If you buy foods in bulk when the item is in good supply and therefore reduced in price, the savings can be enormous. The twenty-five to fifty percent savings on the purchase of items you need represents a wise investment when you compare that return to what your money would be earning in a bank. A word of caution: Just because the store display tells you that something is a great deal doesn't mean it's true. Make sure that you can't get the same item for less somewhere else.

Buy rice, beans, flour, and sugar in bags rather than boxes. For convenience, keep smaller containers in your kitchen that you replenish. Be careful, though. You will only save money if you need the items and if you don't eat more by having more on hand. For example, if you buy three gallons of ice cream on sale and eat it all in two weeks, have you really saved?

Having a pantry is clearly essential in this overall strategy. Even though you may not have a separate room for this purpose, you can create one. Turn a section of cupboards in your kitchen into a pantry or install shelves in a nearby closet, in the laundry room, or in the garage.

A separate freezer will allow you to stock up on perishables. You can store meat, poultry, fish, and vegetables you grew yourself or bought at reduced prices at the end of the growing season. By working ahead and freezing, you can prepare convenience meals at a fraction of the cost of storebought. If you live in a rural area, a separate freezer may be a necessity. If you already own one or can buy one secondhand, terrific. If not, consider purchasing your own. A word of caution: The costs of the initial purchase, the electricity to run it, and the risk of spoilage in case of a power outage may outweigh the advantages.

Plan Your Meals

Planning your meals one week or even a month in advance is the best way to cut your food shopping costs. Advance planning not only makes meals cheaper, it rewards you with better, more varied menus. You also avoid the stress of frantically searching for something, *anything*, to fix for dinner. It's highly unlikely that you can come up with a nutritious and economical dinner every night if your planning starts at five P.M. Here are some tips to keep in mind when planning your menus and making your shopping list.

✔ Look at newspaper ads and at what you've got on hand before you plan your meals. Build some of your meals around meat, poultry, and other items that are on special.

✔ Consider leftovers when planning. If you know you're going to fix a bean soup and cornbread dinner using a leftover hambone, buy the cornbread mix and the dried beans (if you don't already have a twenty-five-pound bag in your pantry) when you buy the ham.

✔ If you're cooking a family favorite like lasagna or chili, double the recipe and serve it again to get more than one meal from the one-time preparation.

✔ Be flexible with your menus. If, when shopping, you find an exceptional buy, add meals featuring these specials to your list of menu items.

Plan Your Food Shopping

Once you have your menus ready, go into purchasing agent mode and plan your shopping.

✔ Shop the discount food warehouses for basics. These are usually "no frills" establishments: no music, no fancy displays, and often no baggers. Variety is limited and containers come economy-sized and/or bundled together in one large package. Although frequently quite a distance from home, the consistently low prices are worth the trip. The food warehouses offer all their stock at what normal stores consider "on-sale" prices. Many families find it practical to go to a discount food warehouse once or twice a month at which time they load up the car with as much as it will hold; once a week they shop at their regular grocery stores for perishables.

✔ Regardless of where you shop, try to cut down on the number of trips you make to the store. Cathy, a Colorado homemaker, devotes the better part of Wednesday to shopping. After reading the ads, she drives her "territory" to stock up on sale items; then she does her regular shopping. If you're extremely self-disciplined and selective about what you buy, you can probably get away with shopping twice a week without doing too much damage to the budget.

✔ Use the "buddy system." Before shopping, you and your neighborhood friends can check with each other to see if anyone needs something. In addition to saving time and gas, you can also split a bulk- or economy-sized item that's too big for a single family.

✔ Buy only items on your list. Impulse buys can wreak havoc on your monthly costs. Consider this everyday example: Let's say you take your son and daughter shopping every week. He always talks you into potato chips and dip; she always begs you for the latest and greatest cereal or snack food she has seen advertised on television. And you yourself can't resist the shortcakes tucked temptingly next to the strawberries! At today's prices, we're easily talking seven dollars. A year later, fifty-two weeks of this—and let's face it, an estimate of seven dollars' worth of impulse purchases is on the low side—you've racked up $364 worth of unneeded food. Worse yet, it is food that is loaded with sugar or fat and very little nutritional value. One of the lessons here? Shop alone when you can.

✔ Be aware of "grocery store psychology." Many grocers stock the lower shelves, which are easier to reach, with sweets; foods that tempt children often surround the check-out stands.

✔ Buy produce in season. Never buy the first crop; prices will go lower. When prices on an item have hit rock bottom—often at the end of the growing season—this is the time to stock up. Either freeze it or have an old-fashioned canning weekend to take advantage of your favorite produce so you can enjoy it throughout the year.

✔ Buy fruits and vegetables from stands, from open markets, or from the farms and orchards themselves. You'll save the mark-up the warehousers and grocers add to the price.

✔ Beware of packaged fresh produce. Stores package fresh fruits and vegetables in order to trick you into buying more than you need and/or to hide flawed goods.

✔ Select apples, peaches, and other fruit with the eater in mind. For example, why give a small child a large peach when a small one is all he or she can eat and the rest will be wasted?

✔ Check out the quality of generic or store brands and buy them when possible. The price difference between a national name brand and the generic brand is often quite substantial.

✔ Use unit pricing. By law many stores tell you the price per pound or per cup on shelf tags. Compare different brands and sizes to see which is the best buy. I have sometimes found the larger size to be higher in price per unit.

✔ Study the ingredient labels. What you see first is what you get the most of. Reading labels is a pain but can be worth it. Why? In this way you can direct your food dollar toward foods that will do you the most good and away from products that consist primarily of water, sugar, and chemicals. As the old dictum goes, if you can't pronounce it, you probably shouldn't be eating it.

✔ Coupons can save you money if you are systematic about using them. They are especially profitable if you use them in a store that gives you double their printed worth. But it's important to remember that you can also lose money if you get something with a coupon that family members don't like, or if you buy an item that is more expensive than another brand even after you deduct the coupon savings.

✔ If your family drinks wine, buy it by the case or on sale for savings of ten percent or more. For table wines, try out the variety that sells by the half-gallon or gallon, or try the "box wines" that chill conveniently in refrigerator.

Prepare Foods That Stretch Your Food Dollar

✔ Breastfeed your baby. Powdered formula costs eight dollars per week; prepared formula costs astronomically more. Breastfeeding costs literally pennies a day and provides a superior diet to boot.

✔ Make your own foods whenever possible. The cost of one slice of store-bought peach pie may be double the cost of a home-baked pie. Women

who buy convenience foods are paying for what
Sylvia Porter calls "built-in maid service." You
pay to have someone wrap up individual
servings. You pay to have someone add water
to your condensed soup. You pay to have
someone sugar the cereal or add dry fruit. You
pay to have someone season your rice and
butter your beans. And your built-in maid
probably doesn't season the food to your taste
or serve portions that fill up everyone. (Once in
a great while, however, this rule doesn't stand.
For example, it's cheaper to buy cornbread mix
than it is to make it from scratch.)

✔ Eliminate waste. If you have leftover cottage
cheese—a perennial problem in my
refrigerator—use it to replace ricotta cheese in
lasagna, or in certain tuna casseroles. Have a
"leftover night" or a no-grocery week so that
you will be forced to search back in the
cupboard for those long-forgotten cans of
chicken, sardines, clam chowder, or pumpkin.

✔ Use leftovers in school lunches for a nice change
of pace from sandwiches.

✔ Save money with nonfat dry milk. It contains
large amounts of protein at very little cost. If
you or your family doesn't like the taste, mix it
with whole milk or use it in desserts, soups, etc.

✔ Dilute ready-made salad dressings. You don't
need all that oil and the taste will be more
subtle, therefore better. Dilute frozen juices to
make them go farther.

✔ Use leftover meats in casseroles.

✔ Treat meat as a side dish, even a condiment,
rather than the main attraction. Casseroles,
main dish salads, soups, stews, and stir-fries

enable you to play up vegetables and grains and minimize meat. Develop a repertoire of meatless main dishes.

✔ Serve steaming bowls of oatmeal or homemade granola for breakfast rather than more expensive ready-to-eat cereals.

✔ Pack popcorn for lunches as well as for after-school snacks. Unbuttered popcorn is healthy, economical, delicious, and low in calories.

By working a food shopping "system," grocery shopping becomes less of a chore and more of a challenge, a contest of wits in which you try to beat regular store prices while at the same time feeding your family foods that are healthier and more delicious than ever.

How to Save When You Shop for Clothes

Unlike grocery shopping, clothes shopping is a form of recreation for me. When I'm shopping for clothes, the T-shirt slogans proclaiming, "I was born to shop" or "Shop till you drop" or "I'd rather be at the mall" start to make sense. The excitement of entering a store and surveying the racks and displays of things I might buy, things that will make me look and feel good, never gets old.

Although we at-home mothers don't need the high-powered wardrobes many of us wore at work, we do need, perhaps more than ever, to feel attractive. Clothes are an important element in the image we project to others and how we perceive ourselves. But here's the dilemma: We need to buy clothes to enhance our appearance; we also need more and more clothes for our growing family. But—wouldn't you know it?—we have less money with which we can buy that increasing number of clothes. What to do? This section provides hope. If you follow these tips, you will slash your clothing costs *and* be better dressed than ever!

Plan Your and Your Family's Wardrobe

Before you shop, take a wardrobe inventory. Invite a friend to help you; a fresh set of eyes will be better able to spot cute new combinations, or potential candidates for your next garage sale. Here are a few tips to help you with this process:

- ✔ To weed out garments unworthy of closet space, use the three year rule: If you haven't worn it in three years, pitch it. Things do come back in style, but they usually come back with different cuts and details.

- ✔ For your inventory of clothes to keep, take a sheet of paper and at the top write out these headings: Workout, Casual, Dressy-Casual, Dressy, Formal. Now make a list of complete outfits you have in each category. Make sure you include accessories you plan to wear such as scarves, jewelry, belt, purse, socks, and shoes. For example, under "Casual," you might list: jeans with white turtleneck sweater, designer sweatshirt, sneakers. If you plan to wear regular socks and no special accessories, don't list them. However, if you were going to dress up the jeans, list the following under "Dressy Casual": white blouse, leather belt, gold earrings, navy print socks, loafers, navy wool blazer and gold pin. Use your imagination to come up with as many attractive combinations as you can.

- ✔ Make a list of clothes and accessories you need and another list of what you would love to have. As you add pieces to your wardrobe, try to build your wardrobe around a few basic colors. Concentrate on separates so you can mix and match the different color-coordinated garments for different looks.

✔ When planning purchases, put versatile, year-round garments high on your list. For example, buy a tailored tweed sports jacket (bought off the clearance rack for practically nothing, of course!) that goes with your jeans, your pants, and a dressy skirt. Buy a dress that can be dressed up or dressed down for different occasions.

Comedian Henry Cho once remarked to his girlfriend when she asked him to go shopping with her, "If I want to be around clothes that have never been worn, I'll sit in your closet for an hour." Keep your inventory lists handy, and you'll be less likely to have a closet stuffed full of clothes, yet "nothing to wear." Most importantly, having a list will help you be ready to pounce on a good bargain for those things you need when you see them. You can then apply whatever you save on those purchases toward the extras you want.

Apply this method to the wardrobes of your other family members to save a bundle.

Shopping for Your Own Wardrobe: Today's clothing stores, especially the discount stores where you will be spending most of your time, often consist of rows and rows of clothes racks tended by a lone salesperson at a mobbed cash register. Helpful, fashion-conscious salespeople, able to dole out sage advice, seem to be a thing of the past. Nowadays, you need to know exactly what you want and be willing to root through the racks to find it. Having your list helps, as does having a record of other family members' sizes—chest, waist, dress and pant inseam.

✔ Buy clothes off-season to achieve dramatic savings. Take your list of clothing items which you know you need or will be needing in the next six to twelve months. When end-of-the-season clearance sales come along, or when a store offers a special sale, or better yet, when even those items are reduced again, buy what you need for the coming year. This one tip can save you up to fifty percent of your total clothes budget.

✔ Shop off-price stores, bargain stores, factory outlets, and clearance stores, where you can get first-quality merchandise at substantial savings.

✔ Don't be afraid of buying returns or irregulars at factory outlet stores. The flaws are usually so minor that it doesn't matter. I once purchased an expensive white blouse at considerable savings simply because it was slightly soiled. After one washing, it looked like new.

✔ Examine the quality—it varies widely—of clothing at discount stores such as Target and Wal-Mart. Avoid poor quality garments. Poor quality clothes "go bad" quickly. After washing, they sag, shrink, droop, and/or wrinkle. Basically, they look cheap.

✔ Mail-order catalogues, frequently offering excellent quality for reasonable prices, have on-sale sections and will take returns.

✔ Check into local thrift and secondhand shops. You can sell your clothes on consignment there and can also buy next-to-new quality clothes at very low prices. Before shopping a thrift store or garage sale, make sure you have your list of family members' measurements and a tape measure in your purse.

✔ When you shop, go straight to the sales tables and racks. This way, you won't be tempted by clothing you can't afford. As the saying goes,

"What the eye doesn't see, the heart doesn't grieve after."

✔ Make a clothing list and a budget and stick to it. Refer to the list of outfits you already have. If you need a light jacket, don't veer off into the shoe department and buy a pair of summer sandals. If you feel yourself heading for an unwise purchase, give yourself the time-out treatment described earlier (page 109).

✔ Buy certain items in quantity. For example, buy three pairs of matching panty hose. You can cut one leg out of a pair when it runs, then one leg out of another when it runs. Wear both pairs of panty hose, each with one good leg to equal two good legs for a matched set. Apply the same principle to socks. Buy knee highs and socks in the same color and style. When one wears out or disappears, you can mate it with a sock from another pair.

✔ Before purchasing an item, consider the cost of its care, particularly dry cleaning. For example, the cost of drycleaning a nonwashable light-colored suit which may need cleaning after one or two wearings, could, in no time, amount to more than the original cost of the suit.

✔ When buying one item, consider what else you will need to complete the outfit. If you find a great dress on sale for twenty dollars but you need a pair of shoes, a purse, earrings, colored hose and a belt to go with it, where is your bargain?

✔ Direct more of your clothing dollars toward everyday clothes, which will wear longer and can be cared for more easily. If you're going to pay for good fabric and tailoring, do so when you know you will wear the item often.

✔ Avoid faddish clothes. If you have to have something that will be passé next year, make sure you get a real bargain on it. Classic styles will be better additions to your wardrobe.

✔ If the shoes don't fit, don't buy. If they are not comfortable within the first five minutes in the store, they probably won't be comfortable after you've worn them all day. Don't let a salesperson convince you the pain will go away once they're "broken in."

✔ Don't buy skin-tight garments on the assumption that you are about ready to lose fifteen pounds.

✔ Always save your sales slip. In many stores you cannot get a refund without it.

✔ If you get stung on a purchase (for example, a dress that bleeds dye onto the white collar even when washed according to instructions), go back to the store and complain. If you do not get satisfaction, go to the manager. Keep going until you are satisfied.

Shopping for Your Children's Wardrobe:

✔ Beware of cheap shoes. They can turn out to be the most expensive shoes of all. If, after a week of wear, the sole starts peeling off, you have to go shoe shopping again. Some stores guarantee that their shoes won't wear out: if they wear out before your child outgrows them, the store replaces them.

✔ Children's feet are developing, so make sure their shoes fit correctly. Don't pass shoes on from one child to the next unless you're sure the shoes are the correct size.

✔ Take note of what your children like to wear before shopping for them. Let them look through the ads with you in order to prevent wasting time and money shopping for clothes they will refuse to wear.

✔ Shop the garage sales for great buys on children's clothes. Children's egos won't be damaged by wearing secondhand clothes—at least until they become teenagers. Remember to take your list of measurements and a tape measure.

✔ Don't buy too many clothes. Drawers stuffed with clothes are difficult to keep organized. Buy good, durable things, only fewer of them.

✔ Buy clothes with built-in growth features such as deep hems and cuffs, adjustable straps on overalls and jumpers, and elastic waistbands. Always buy clothes as well as shoes with a little "room to grow."

✔ Remember to save clothes for brothers and sisters or make exchanges with other families. Good quality children's clothes can last through two or three children.

How to Save When You Shop for Gifts

Birthday gifts, holiday gifts, graduation and wedding gifts, shower gifts, teacher and coach gifts, hostess gifts—the number of gifts we purchase each year is astonishing. Watch the magazines for creative ideas for home-made gifts. For the rest, buy in advance. Make a list of all the gifts you anticipate buying in the next six months to a year. When you're on the shopping trail and you spot a bargain, jump on it. Your treasure trove of gifts will save you tons of money and time!

One thing is clear: It pays to be a bargain hunter. Once you've shopped the sales and know the thrill of the "kill"— finding top quality merchandise at rock bottom prices—you'll never want to pay full retail again. It's not necessary or even desirable to follow meticulously, from A to Z, all the tips and strategies in this chapter. You'd have time for nothing else but shopping and you'd drive yourself crazy. However, you can pick out a few of these strategies and follow them systematically and consistently. Cutting your costs in this way means conquering an increasingly complex marketplace, that "discount jungle," by virtue of your own knowledge, know-how, and initiative. Happy hunting! May you never pay full retail again!

Exercises for Helping You Shop Smarter

1. Rate yourself as a shopper on a scale of 5 (you are a confirmed bargainhunter) to 1 (you never ask the price of anything).

2. Analyze your current food shopping practices. Where do you shop? How often? How much do you usually spend on each trip? Do you plan meals?

3. How much do you currently spend on groceries per month? How much do you think you could save?

4. What food shopping strategies do you currently use? List at least three.

5. What changes could you make to start saving more money on your food bill? List at least three.

6. Analyze your current clothes shopping patterns. Where do you shop? What condition is your wardrobe in right now? How much do you usually spend for clothes in a year? Do you ever shop the end-of-season sales? Do you usually pay full price? What clothes do you need? What clothes would you like to have?

7. What money-saving strategies do you currently use to save on clothes? List at least three.

8. What strategies can you adopt to save even more on your clothing bills? List at least three.

Part Three

On Your Own

9

The Home Alone Syndrome

The condition of being home alone has features which
are inherently depressing to people, regardless of age,
sex, personality, or socioeconomic status. Being at home
alone without interaction with other adults can
precipitate depression in those who previously
functioned well. It can also exacerbate an already
existing depression.

— Lois Kalafus[1]

Lois Kalafus' thesis is quite simple: Anyone who's
home alone for a prolonged period is likely to get depressed.
She analyzes the factors that contribute to making being home
alone inherently depressing and suggests possible "treat-
ments" of these external environmental conditions.

Her concept struck an immediate chord in me. I was
relieved to finally have a clear "diagnosis" for the pessimistic
period I experienced following the birth of my third daughter,
Elizabeth. After deciding to take an indefinite hiatus from

---

[1] In a presentation to the Association of Clinical Social Workers
Conference, San Francisco, May 28, 1992.

teaching high school German, I found myself unprepared for the emotional "pits" that I experienced for the next year or so—way past the postpartum blues that I had expected.

This book, in fact, found its beginnings in my search for an explanation for what I now believe was my bout with the Home Alone Syndrome. After I bounced back, my normal self-confidence and cheerfulness restored, I remained intrigued by the phenomenon. Was I alone in this experience? What were the causes? What factors enabled me to feel happy and fulfilled once more? The content of this book is largely a product of the answers I found to these questions. One thing became clear: Experiencing some form of the Home Alone Syndrome appears to be an occupational hazard of at-home motherhood in the '90s.

What's in a Name?

The name "Home Alone Syndrome" and the concept it describes offer a practical and common-sensical way of looking at many of the emotional challenges at-home mothers face today. I like it for three reasons.

First of all, the philosophy of the Home Alone Syndrome reframes the problem of depression (the more standard but not quite as accurate term for the Home Alone Syndrome) from "What's wrong with me (or them)?" to "What's wrong with the situation?" To me, this is much less frightening than putting ourselves or our families "on the couch" (though seeking therapy, however frightening it may seem, is sometimes necessary). Overbearing husbands, unsupportive parents, demanding children—all are unfortunately very real. Postpartum hormonal disturbances are an added factor. However, according to Kalafus, the postpartum blues are also related to the Home Alone Syndrome. Otherwise, how do we explain the fact that adoptive mothers also experience "postpartum" depression? (Dix 118) But while we can do little to change our own hormone production, significant others in our lives, or society as a whole, we can change our lifestyles in ways that mitigate the severity of the Home Alone Syndrome.

Secondly, the philosophy of the Home Alone Syndrome is inclusive—everybody's invited—regardless of age, gender, or socioeconomic status. Kalafus says, "some are retired, some are out of work due to illness or disability, some are housewives or new mothers, and some are unemployed or laid off." Rocket scientists and rollerblade artists, men and women, young and old alike are vulnerable.

The third and best thing about the philosophy of the Home Alone Syndrome is that having a case of it does not mean we're crazy, weak-minded, or going "mad" as in *The Diary of a Mad Housewife*. Most people who suffer from the Home Alone Syndrome are mentally healthy and have had no complaints until they started staying at home full-time.

Who's at Risk for the Home Alone Syndrome?

"Alone!? I'd give my right arm for five little minutes to myself." If you think your two talkative toddlers disqualify you as a candidate for the Home Alone Syndrome, they don't. Kalafus defines being alone as spending most or all of the day apart from others with whom we can talk *on our level*. Thus, it is entirely possible to feel lonely and alienated even though we're surrounded with the pitter and patter of much-loved little feet and voices. That puts most at-home mothers squarely at risk.

On an intuitive level, most at-home mothers are aware of a link between staying home full-time and depression. Most of us have navigated those rough waters to pull ourselves up to secure emotional ground on the other side, but we all know women who still haven't made it. We don't like to admit our bouts of depression; we prefer to keep silent. We don't want to be like the bored and "trapped" housewives of yesteryear, whom Betty Friedan described in her famous line: "the sad housewife with the problem that has no name." Most of us certainly aren't "trapped"; we had to fight tooth and nail to claim our right to leave the workforce to come home. If anything, many of us felt trapped on the dual-income treadmill.

And yet, we are sometimes sad. We weren't prepared to be tossed and buffeted by our emotions; we had expected ourselves to execute a smooth landing and are perhaps ashamed of our poor performance. We often grossly underestimate the emotional adjustments we need to make in order to feel as happy at home as we had hoped. Many of us never stopped to wonder how our self-confidence and identity would hold up after giving up something that was so precious to us—our careers—to stay home alone.

If we think about men's traditional roles, we can understand more clearly the inevitable cause and effect of leaving the workforce to stay home alone and the inner crisis it precipitates. Consider the man who has worked hard at his job all of his life. He resigns from the corporation where he worked for fifteen years because, oh, let's say, he wants to write a book, retrain himself in desktop publishing, and spend more time with his family. We would fully expect this man to undergo a period of unsettling stress during which time he will experience anxieties about his ability and his identity. In other words, we expect him to experience the Home Alone Syndrome.

Women are no different. We are not automatically programmed to adjust to full-time domestic life. Some women never become depressed, but most women do experience some form of depression as a result of being at home alone. In most cases this means mild and fleeting periods of the blues, although for an unfortunate few, it can mean a full-scale clinical depression that needs professional treatment. Some women are conscious of their depression; others are unaware of it until they have already climbed out of the well and can look back. Fortunately, the Home Alone Syndrome is usually confined to the transition period lasting between three or four months to a year. Once a new mother or retiree figures out ways to reduce the negative features of staying home alone, the depression dissipates.

Throughout the rest of this chapter, we will continue to look at the Home Alone Syndrome and how it might be relevant to your situation. By preparing for the normal, predictable emotional stages we commonly experience, we can reduce the impact of the three main factors which contribute to the Home Alone Syndrome:

1. Isolation

2. Lack of Structure

3. Loss of Identity

Isolation

For many of us, before we came home full-time, our lives were too busy; we spent long hours at work and took meals out at restaurants. Sometimes our homes felt more like "crashpads," places to refuel, get clean clothes, and fall gratefully and exhaustedly into bed. Being at home full-time, the situation is reversed: we spend long, quiet hours in not-so-splendid isolation and frequently long to "get out."

Although we may feel a sense of relief at having the house to ourselves after the rest of the household bustles off to work or school, a sinking sensation at being left behind may follow. Kalafus reports that many of her clients complain of feeling like they are "stuck" and "spinning their wheels."

These feelings are largely caused by the lack of feedback. Negative thinking flourishes in isolation. With no one to bounce ideas off of, no one to distract us from our own ruminations, no one to challenge us or affirm us, it's easy to get absorbed in our own feelings, worries, and fantasies.

For example, a woman at home alone all day with an infant may eagerly await the return of her husband. She is desperate for adult conversation or the chance to get out with him. He, however, exhausted from a long day at work, only wants peace and quiet. She interprets his response as rejection. The next day while he's at work, she may stew and fret, worrying that he's losing interest in her or, worse yet, that he's sharing his work problems with the beautiful (she imagines) new office secretary. To top it off, her toddler accidentally chips his tooth on the bathroom sink. She then berates herself mercilessly, "I can't do anything right! No wonder John isn't interested in me anymore."

In addition, if a person received negative messages in childhood, which can leave residual feelings of inadequacy, isolation reactivates those feelings because of the lack of positive feedback from others. Like Patsy Cline, such a person may "fall to pieces" at the slightest provocation.

Here are four tips to reduce the negative impact of isolation in your life.

1. Make it a point to "get out" every day. Even though taking small children and the requisite equipment, diapers, and food supplies make you feel like you're leading a traveling circus, don't get lazy on this point.

2. Invite somebody over for coffee. The kids can play together while you talk to some grown-ups. Even a short visit can get you out of the doldrums. Socializing is not an elective; it's a required course.

3. Enlist your husband's support. Warn him about possible Home Alone Syndrome and ask him to do his part to prevent a severe case. An extra phone call during a lull at the office, words of appreciation, or lunch once a week (go to a cafeteria-style restaurant that absorbs noises of small children) will help you over the hurdle. Don't feel guilty asking for extra TLC. You deserve it. Remember, you're doing the most important job in the universe.

4. Make a blatant appeal for admiring recognition. On days when you're feeling underappreciated,

underloved and overworked, when you've spent half the day working your buns off and the other half complaining about it, do the following: Tell your family that what you really want besides a little help is to have someone—better yet, all of them—tell you how fabulous they think you are. Go so far as to make suggestions: "How in the world do you do it!?" or "I admire you more than any other woman in the world including (fill in the blank)!" or "I hope I'll be half as good when I'm a mother" or "How do you manage to look so gorgeous when you're doing all that dirty work?" Requested compliments aren't as good as compliments that are volunteered, but they're better than nothing.

Lack of Structure

Get up at six to be ready to leave the house for work by 7:30. Eat lunch at noon; drive home at 5:30. Projects, deadlines, presentations, meetings, reviews, evaluations, promotions—for many of us, the workday structured our lives and provided a sense of purpose for the day.

At home, the baby's nap schedule and the schoolday structure our children's activities and therefore ours. But beyond that, we're on our own. Ah, freedom! Luxurious? Yes. For a while it may even feel like being on vacation. But in time, the lack of structure promotes a feeling of disorganization and even uselessness that is anything but pleasurable.

Of course our day has a purpose. Still, why bother to carefully apply make-up or put a little sizzle in the hairstyle? No one will see us. Why waste time putting together a to-die-for outfit: Ten to one the baby will spit up on it within the hour. Why wait for noon to eat? We're on vacation! We can grab Chips Ahoy and a handful of Ruffles each time of the twenty-five times we come into the kitchen. After a few months of "vacationing," our rapidly expanding bodily structure will more than make up for the lack of structure in our days!

No need to apply ourselves diligently to our projects around home. Who's to know? There are no performance evaluations or promotions given here. Nobody will give us an "A" for effort at parenting. Furthermore, there are no standards, no clearly defined set of expectations for how the job should be performed. We are our own judges. Unfortunately, this means we never know for sure how we're doing.

Most people have never been trained to structure their own lives. First parents, then the schools, then work have provided structure for us. For the first time, we're our own boss. And as they say, it gets lonely at the top. Four strategies for restructuring your new life at home follow.

Give Yourself Something to Look Forward To

One fine summer afternoon over grilled hamburgers, my wise neighbor Larry was kind enough to share his philosophy of happiness with me. Borrowing a bit from Freud, he said he believes people need three things to be happy: meaningful work, someone to love, and something to look forward to. I thought to myself that at-home mothers have the first two locked up, but that the critical third part of Larry's happiness triad—something to look forward to—is sometimes missing. Therefore, at-home mothers need to consciously incorporate some concrete things to look forward to into our lives.

Spend some time with your husband planning special activities—a special romantic dinner at a restaurant you've been wanting to try; a weekend at the beach or in the mountains; a family reunion. Your special activity doesn't need to happen this weekend; it can be way off in the future and still work its magic on your attitude. When you start feeling like your life is as dull as dishwater, focus on the next thing that's coming up. Think about what you'll need to pack, or go to the library and get information about the area you'll be visiting. Just planning what you'll need to do to get ready can lift your drooping spirits.

Join a Group That Meets Regularly

Kalafus notes that it is sometimes difficult to keep drumming up new activities to participate in. Try signing up for a class or joining a club or civic organization that meets regularly. Then you just need to fill in the appropriate times on your calendar and put notes like "get a sitter for class."

Make a Daily "To Do" List on a Calendar

Write down all the things you hope to accomplish in a day. Include even seemingly inconsequential items like getting dressed, bathing and dressing the baby, eating lunch, calling the plumber, weeding the garden, grocery shopping, or doing a load (or ten) of laundry. Next, write down something that you want to do: perhaps read a chapter of a good novel, get together with or phone a friend or relative, plan your summer wardrobe, or take a walk. At the end of the day, when you have checked off all the items, you will have tangible proof of how productive you really are. Kalafus suggests this technique as a good way to get in the habit of creating our own structure, deadlines and so on.

Set Your Own Standards

Call a meeting for yourself (there is, after all, no other adult home to attend) and review some of the items you wrote down on your mission statements in chapters 1 through 4. Use these as a set of standards by which you can judge yourself. Every few weeks, haul them out and see how you're doing. For example, if in chapter 1, you wrote as one of your mission statements that you intended to do something special with your child every day, see if you've really been doing that. Or, if you have decided that you want to limit your daytime TV viewing to an hour a day (perhaps you decided on this goal when you realized the tube had not had a chance to cool down in weeks), you can evaluate your success. In this way, you are at least accountable to yourself.

Loss of Identity

Right or wrong, society defines people by what they do. One of the first questions on any routine questionnaire is "Occupation" or "Place of Employment." The first question that comes up at a cocktail party is, "What do you do?" or "Where do you work?" Your work may have been a high-powered career for which you trained long and hard; or it may have been the start of a career or even just a holding pattern until marriage and motherhood. Regardless, for many at-home mothers, our jobs gave us a sense of identity; it told others where we fit in.

If your job represented a significant part of your life, you are bound to experience the loss of that job and the relationships that went along with it, with all the attendant anxiety and even grief. Disoriented without familiar roles and structures, you may feel like Alice in Wonderland when the Caterpillar pointed to her contemptuously saying, "You! Who *are* you?" This is only natural. After all, you're changing "stories" right in mid-book and you haven't quite figured out all the new characters and their roles, especially your own!

For at-home mothers, eventually our loss becomes our gain. Piece by piece, we redefine ourselves with new activities, new relationships, new interests and affiliations, new projects and accomplishments. We learn we have a lot more to offer the world than a job description. Our new, broader identity relates more to what we really *are*—all of our qualities, thoughts, and deeds—rather than to what we *do*.

I want to emphasize here that this is not an overnight process, no matter how much we want it to be. The adjustment time varies from woman to woman and is often determined by how much work she puts into the process. The more acute stages of the Home Alone Syndrome are usually over by a year, but often it takes several years before we are truly as fulfilled and excited about our life at home as we want to be. As we regain our inner security and confidence, we are able to value the work we do at home as much as we should. The opinion of others becomes less significant to us. When we look to ourselves and other like-minded individuals to authenticate our experiences at home, we will no longer feel that we are playing second fiddle to the career-oriented Superwoman.

In the meantime, we keep rebuilding. Many of us may still look wistfully at the exciting lives our working counterparts seem to lead. We may occasionally feel that our old identities were somehow better than our new personas. Yes, we have given up some things to stay home to raise children—but not forever. In many ways, toughing it out in this in-between period is a true litmus test of our characters and capabilities and courage.

"And What Do *You* Do?"

In the meantime, we have to deal with the public. We want to project the self-confidence that we aspire to but haven't quite reached yet. We know our hearts will catch up in due time. It's important to prepare for the inevitable "What do you do?" Otherwise, you may find yourself acting embarrassed, your heart sinking, horrified at hearing yourself murmuring apologetically, "Nothing. I'm just a housewife." Such an answer won't do! After all, it doesn't reflect your true feelings, does it? You are proud to be able to practice full-time the most important profession in the universe, so show it! Decide what your answer will be, and when you give it, answer with pride.

But how do you express it, exactly? It's tricky. The semantics of the situation are sticky; there is no perfect answer. Saying you're a housewife or homemaker is somehow inadequate. It puts too much emphasis on being married to a house and on doing domestic chores, and too little emphasis on the main event: raising children.

Euphemisms like "home manager" or "domestic engineer" sound silly and pretentious. More creative job descriptions like one I read recently ("a non-invasive brain surgeon"—she instills values and memories in her children's brains) are sure to stimulate interesting conversation, but, like the euphemisms, they send the false message that our job needs to be "dolled up," when we all know that it stands on its own merits, thank you very much.

I prefer the honesty of my friend Susan's answer. "I stay home with the kids," she answers cheerfully and with as much inner dignity as she can muster. Susan, mother of two teenagers, is a freelance writer on the side but because she feels that her main priority is taking care of her children, her answer reflects that priority. Often, however, this answer is a conversational dead-end. To get things going, she fills in with a description of her latest article, the boards she sits on, and the tutoring she does at her son's school. She squeezes in her ballet classes, the Tuesday afternoon jaunts to the beach, the latest art exhibits she has taken her kids to, and her cutting garden. She said to me, eyes twinkling, "I know it's not fair—I keep painting pretty word pictures until they're consumed with envy."

What if the Home Alone Syndrome Lingers?

Since isolation, lack of structure and loss of identity pose a new and unexpected challenge for all of us, the struggle to cope with these issues may well temporarily affect our self-confidence. Kalafus differentiates self-confidence from self-esteem. Self-esteem has to do with one's basic self-liking ("I am a good person worth liking"); self-confidence, however, is a belief in one's own capabilities ("I think I can do it"). Self-confidence allows us to try new things and take risks. Even a person with normally high self-esteem can suffer a deterioration in self-confidence as a result of a prolonged period of isolation.

For example, Jolene, a California homemaker, recalls that once, when she was in her Home Alone phase, she actually panicked at the thought of cooking her favorite Madeira beef recipe for her husband's boss. Although she had prepared the dish at least ten times before, "the recipe seemed so complicated, stuffing the beef, making the wine sauce and the side dishes, doing everything just so, I was overwhelmed at the details."

These crises of confidence are natural responses to adjusting to a new lifestyle. Women who have just moved to a new area and who are having their first baby are especially at risk. As stated earlier, most women bounce back after a few months to a year. However, sometimes, the sad feelings persist and symptoms of a full-scale depression may set in. Irritability, sleep problems, restlessness, feelings of hopelessness and pessimism, fatigue, weight loss or gain, an inability to concentrate, and, perhaps, thoughts of suicide or death are all symptoms of clinical depression. Kalafus lists three more extreme symptoms that the Home Alone Syndrome can lead to. These are substance abuse, hypochondria, and agoraphobia, a fear of going out of the house.

If you feel your blues or other symptoms have gone beyond what is normal, talk to your physician and/or friends about a referral for professional counseling. Just make sure you get a counselor who understands the special issues of being a new mother and being a mother at home. Some therapists see depression as caused by a woman's failure to adjust to the mothering role, or they see serious pathology where there is none. Don't be embarrassed. Fortunately, just like arthritis and high blood pressure, depression responds to treatment. Though it may be difficult to ask for help when you're depressed, it's essential that you do.

Home Remedies

Happily, the clinical social workers who gathered at their annual meeting liked Lois' theory, too. They applauded their approval; several therapists made a point of telling her they would now be on the lookout for patients at high risk for the Home Alone Syndrome.

As for the rest of us who are at risk and who plan to manage our own mental health care, forewarned is forearmed.

Knowing what could happen, we can practice some home remedies, measures that work to combat the impact of the isolation, the lack of structure, and the loss of identity that are in themselves depressing.

Our success in shortening or avoiding the symptoms of the Home Alone Syndrome depends in large part upon our willingness to seek out a reinforcing group of people to replace our work groups, to restructure our lives with new goals and standards so that we are at least accountable to ourselves, and to redefine ourselves by new personal and intellectual interests. The adjustment process takes more than just sitting in front of our favorite soap, waiting for the adjustment period to pass. Remember that the same thoughts come to most women at home alone; it's what you *do* about them during the adjustment period that makes the difference, not just the time itself.

The next five chapters are devoted to concrete and practical ways to help you keep moving in the right direction—that is, away from conditions that promote the onset of the Home Alone Syndrome. We will explore useful and exciting ways to exchange potential Home Alone Syndrome feelings of loneliness, aimlessness and uselessness for feelings of belongingness, purposefulness and productiveness. In the process of designing our own remedies to work through the challenges that at-home mothers face today, we grow in maturity and health. We find that indeed, we *can* go home again and find the happiness, fulfillment and identity there that we always wanted.

Exercises for Becoming Comfortable at Home Alone

1. Describe any negative emotions you feel about being an at-home mother.

2. If you worked before, how emotionally invested were you in your job? What do you miss most about that job?

3. When you are alone with your thoughts and feelings, what most frequently goes through your mind about not having a job outside the home?

4. How much time every day do you spend in contact with other adults? Do you feel you have enough adult contact? Do you ever feel lonely? What steps could you take to reduce your isolation? List at least three.

5. Describe a typical day in your life. Be specific. What items would usually be found on your "To Do" list? What "want" items would be there? Which would you like to add?

6. What do you do to combat the blues or to keep your sanity?

7. Do you find yourself making negative, self-defeating statements to yourself during the day? Describe them in a few sentences.

8. What can you do to cut back on playing these negative tapes?

9. Describe your response at social gatherings when someone asks you, "Do you work?"

10. Write out a "press release statement" you can plan to give as your response to the question, "What do you do?"

11. Do you currently write a "To Do" list and/or a calendar?

12. Think of the mission exercises you wrote out earlier in this book. Use those mission statements and new ones to generate a list of ten

items to be used as a set of standards for which you could be accountable (for example, doing something special with your child every day, quitting smoking, getting exercise every day, limiting TV).

13. What event are you currently looking forward to? List three other potential activities that would qualify as something to look forward to.

14. Have you added new activities, new relationships, or new interests in an attempt to build up a new identity at home? If so, name them. If not, what would you like them to be?

15. In what ways has staying at home helped you develop or in any way changed you for the better as a person?

10

Finding Your Passion

If you observe a really happy man you find him
building a boat, writing a symphony, educating his son,
growing double dahlias in his garden, or looking for
dinosaur eggs in the Gobi Desert.

— Thomas Wolfe

Anne Morrow Lindbergh wrote in her book *Gifts from
the Sea* about the rejuvenating power of "the time, the quiet,
the peace, to let the pitcher fill up to the brim." If we wait on
our husbands and children hand and foot and tend to every
friend who knocks on the door, we will be drained of our
energy and won't have the inner resources to be truly useful
to others. If, however, we take some time for ourselves, Lindbergh writes, "life rushes back into the void, richer, more vivid,
fuller than before....One is whole again" (39).

If today's at-home mother is to feel whole and happy, she
must take the time to develop talents and interests outside the
context of her family. The concept isn't new. Feminists have
been preaching for years that a woman has a personal obligation to keep developing during all phases of life, including the

childrearing years. This way her self-esteem and independence are not compromised by marriage and children.

I believe that taking the time to develop these talents and outside interests presents the biggest challenge to at-home mothers today. How can we change and grow and develop as people in our own right while adapting to the ever-evolving, ever-changing needs of our families? It doesn't sound easy, and it's not. Finding a mission of your own involves three steps:

1. making the time

2. deciding what you wish to do with the time

3. making it all happen

The stakes are high. If we fail to find ways to develop our own talents and skills at home, we may begin to feel trapped. Feeling trapped, many of us may head back to work before we or our children are really ready. Then everybody loses.

Making the Time

Fortunately, life on the homefront offers the flexibility, time, and freedom to meet this big challenge. At home you have the chance to pursue old and new interests, discarding those that you don't enjoy. You can strike out in several directions before settling on one or two that will remain a central focus in your life. Now is your chance to explore and discover new dimensions within yourself—a chance full-time employment precludes.

Deciding What You Wish to Do

There are so many possibilities, it's sometimes hard to chose what to do first. Creative work is particularly enticing. Working on home projects—sewing new curtains for the nursery, refinishing an antique dresser, designing an herb garden, creating a wall hanging or a short story—not only restores the inner self as all creative work does, but it also provides something tangible to show for your time. This is a real bonus for an at-home mother whose job is notorious for long-term, intangible rewards.

This is your opportunity to get serious about a long-time hobby. Homes can become workshops where women refine their skills in painting, needlecraft, writing, calligraphy, pottery—the list is endless. Some hobbies may later become second careers. A Brownie leader who cut her teeth on the fundamentals of jewelry-making while helping her troop fulfill a badge requirement now has her own line of Indian motif earrings; a grade school art volunteer who designed the T-shirts for the local Fun Run now runs a successful graphic arts business.

My neighbor, Helen MacPherson, was a school teacher before she quit to stay home and raise her two sons. On a lark she took a photography course at a nearby junior college and discovered she was good at it. She turned her guest bathroom into a darkroom and by stages developed herself into a world class photographic artist. A book of her photographs has been published; her last exhibit was at the Singapore Museum of Art.

If you've always had a passion for European history or nineteenth-century literature, your path is clear. While Jane Sommer stayed home to raise her four daughters, she nurtured her interest in pre-Colombian art by reading articles and books on the subject and volunteering as a docent at the Denver Museum of Natural History. When the family planned a vacation, she lobbied for Mexico. Over the years she filled nooks and crannies of her home with shards of water vessels, tiny cat gods, and other pre-Colombian artifacts she collected on digs there. At fifty-five she launched her last daughter off to college and rolled up her sleeves to work hard on her own mission: a PhD in archaeology. She is now a curator at the museum where she once volunteered. Jane doesn't think the time she spent "indulging" her passion was a waste. Far from it. The time actually helped the information seep in to a deeper level.

Now is the time to research in-depth a topic that interests you. Write a research paper to use later in a class or as a feature for a local newspaper. Local history can be exciting. Interview old timers, scout out museums and write up what you find. Trace your family roots and work your family tree into a wall decoration.

Your passion may be to keep up in a field that you plan to return to someday. Maintaining contacts, reading literature in your field or retraining may be your extracurricular passion in life. You may want to prepare for a change to a new field or to a new aspect of a similar field. Volunteer work that offers practice ground for job-related skills like writing, selling, or public speaking can come in handy later.

Now is the time to acquire tennis or golf or bridge skills that will last a lifetime. Reading or writing books, trying your hand at different craft kits, learning to use the software that has been sitting around unused in the computer for five years, or taking a Spanish course or financial planning workshop are all fun ways to feel productive on your own.

If your interests are unclear, don't panic. If you don't know what you want for yourself, make it your mission to explore your options and ultimately decide on one. However, do not postpone this "just for you" time for later when you might happen to stumble across something that lights your fire. If you've even "half-an-idea" to try something, do it.

Here are some additional ideas that might spark your interest:

Painting (oils, acrylics, watercolor)	Golf, tennis, jogging, horseback riding
Repairing bikes	Leather tooling
Embroidery	Stained glass
Crewel	Carpentry
Needlepoint	Dollhouses
Weaving	Furniture-making

Rug-looming
Centerpieces
Choir
Collages
Christmas decorations
Printing
Calligraphy
Sculpture
Bird houses
Flower & vegetable gardens
Home videos
Bible study group
Landscape waterfalls
Fashion design
Knitting
Scrapbooks
Upholstery
Pillows and drapes
Playing an instrument
Interior decorating
Sewing (clothes, decorative items)
Welding sculptures/ jewelry

Refinishing furniture
Beadwork
Ships in bottles
Jewelry-making
Ceramics
Basket-weaving
Flower arranging
Pottery
Rock collecting/polishing
Fishing, kayaking, canoeing
Kites
Greenhouse gardens
Sketching
Crocheting
Bridge or mah-jong
Taxidermy
Drama
Topiary plants
Music
Metal work
Writing (poetry, stories, children's books)

It doesn't matter what your interest is. What does matter is the feeling of accomplishment, the feeling Lindbergh describes as being "filled to the brim" that results from meaningful activities of your own. By integrating your own passion for something separate from your roles as wife, mother, friend, and so on, at-home motherhood will truly be a personal growth experience. You won't give up anything by staying home. Instead you'll take on new ideas, new experiences, new challenges, new dimensions.

Making It Happen

By completing the following exercises, you will be taking your first few steps toward making your passion happen.

Exercises for Finding Your Passion

1. What do you love? By helping you focus on what you love and love to do, you might be able to see some new avenues of interest open to you. Think about the following:

   a. Is there a subject that always sparked your interest?

   b. What is your personal style? Elements of your personal style (how you dress, how you decorate, the books and magazines you read) provide additional clues for potential interests.

   c. What did you love as a young child? What did you daydream about? Exquisite gowns, hot air balloons, climbing mountains? Are there any skills and talents these early interests point to?

2. List ten positive personal characteristics (e.g., organized, diplomatic, friendly). Do these characteristics suggest any talents or skills worth pursuing? Ask friends to add to the list; often we don't recognize positive qualities in ourselves that are clear to others.

3. If you still don't have a clue as to what your talents, skills and interests are, read Barbara Sher's popular and most excellent book on goal-setting, *Wishcraft*.

4. Write down twenty-five things you want to do before you die. You're brainstorming here, so don't interrupt the free flow of ideas with sordid practicalities. *Think big!* Include things you want to do now and things you want to do later. Write down what you really want no matter how frivolous or selfish or grandiose or banal it might seem. Do not write down what you think you *should* want to do. This is a lust list—not a must list. You want to be a star? A model? To race in the Indy 500? Or, let's get crazy for a minute, you want to operate an earthworm farm? Or maybe you just want a cleaning lady. Write it down. Here's what some others have wished for:

> to play the piano
> to be the next Barbara Walters
> to be an Olympic medalist
> to open a cat boutique
> to speak three foreign languages
> to be president of the PTA
> to be financially independent
> to live in a home furnished by Martha Stewart
> to throw parties catered by Martha Stewart
> to take a cruise every year
> to be on the school board
> to write children's books
> to be a killer bridge player
> to be an aerobics instructor

to be a photo journalist

to be a prominent socialite

to open a pre-school

4. Narrow your list of twenty-five down to ten;
   then to five. Rank them in order of importance
   to you. Decide which mission you want to
   pursue first and write it down.

Congratulations. You've now taken the first step toward making your passion happen. You know where you're going. As the saying goes, "If you don't know where you're going, you'll probably end up somewhere else"; in the case of the at-home mother, you'll end up at home with only the fulfilled dreams of others to show for the time spent there. So, hold that mission in your head, cherish it, nurture it, worry it like a dog does a bone. Never give up. Eventually you'll get there.

In chapter 14, I will show you a technique for breaking down your mission into small, manageable pieces so that you can truly accomplish it. Keep you wish lists as well as your narrowed down mission statements. It's possible—though highly unlikely with small children in the picture—that you'll accomplish several of your missions and be ready to find a new one. Or your mission may need a mid-course adjustment. As Buckminster Fuller once said: How often I saw where I should be going by setting out for somewhere else.

11

Mind over Mush

"Excuse me, did you say something to me?"
"Did I say something?"
"I think so, but I can't remember."

> — Two postpartum mothers
> trying to have a conversation

Judy, thirty-seven-year-old mother of two preschoolers, reports that she started to lose her mental edge as soon as she quit her job as a sales representative for IBM to stay home full-time. She found herself stopping mid-sentence, unable to remember the point she had intended to make. She often failed to find the "right" word to express her thought. Worried that she was developing Alzheimer's, she bought a book on memory enhancement to help fight the mental fog she felt coming over her.

Jean, forty, describes her husband, who appears brisk and shaven at the breakfast table where he reads the paper (uninterrupted), then disappears into the business world. "For twelve hours he's Mr. Communication. He makes all kinds of statements answering tough questions. People hang on his every word. His intellectual powers are skyrocketing. In the meantime...I'm home with the kids....Don't get me wrong, home is where I want to be...but I feel I'm shrinking into an intellectual black hole."

At-home mothers frequently worry about a loss of mental and verbal abilities. Such anxieties are to be expected, reassures Dr. Shirley Feldman, director of Stanford University's Center for the Study of Families. "You sacrifice the intellectual stimulation of the workplace to stay home to nurture and develop your children's minds. There are trade-offs....Working full-time a woman may be stretched so thin her relationships may suffer; conversely, at home she may feel keenly the lack of exciting ideas....This is the downside."

Let's take a closer look at this downside of at-home motherhood and explore three reasons why at-home mothers worry their minds are turning to oatmeal. Then we'll look at some ideas for what you can do about it.

The At-Home Mindset Is Different from the Work Mindset

The focused mindset necessary at work to perform certain jobs doesn't work as well at home. At home a broader, flexible—very flexible—approach works best. This flexibility allows you to carry prioritized lists of overlapping tasks in your head (I'll dust the living room before I pick the kids up from basketball practice, and put the potatoes in the oven before I bathe the baby; I'll get the car out of the shop before I take Joey to the doctor to have his stitches removed).

The at-home mindset encourages interruption. Chances are, you're at home because you want to be the one to bandage Susie's scraped knee or to soothe Bobby's hurt feelings. However, these emergencies always crop up when you least want them to. It's always when you're waxing enthusiastic to a former colleague about your new life that your toddler's high-pitched screaming eventually terminates the conversation, giving your friend the wrong (?) impression.

According to Dr. Feldman, "Even though in theory a woman at home can find the time to accomplish serious work requiring concentration, her interruptibility at home, where she is at the beck and call of her children, makes real progress difficult."

Difficult, but not impossible. Mothers of small children, with the famous eyes in the backs of their heads, can do great things if they develop their peripheral vision, an integral part of the at-home mindset. With one eye she works on her own project; with the other she scans the landscape looking for trouble. She becomes adept at "holding that thought" in order to deal with the emergency of the moment, returning later to take up the thread.

Grown-Up English Becomes a Second Language

The working woman hones her communication skills forty hours a week. Feedback is constant and immediate. Meanwhile, the woman at home with small children is often lucky if she gets an hour a day of English practice. A mother must gear her language down to make herself accessible to her children. However, by exclusively practicing this elementary language used by the family, she may start to lose her ear for formal English.

Julie, a thirty-year-old mother of two pre-schoolers, tells of her horror when she said to her husband as they took a drive in the country, "Fred, look at the horsies!"

Social gatherings, normally considered golden opportunities to practice English conversation, usually find Mom sitting in what Gail Sheehy refers to in her book *Passages* as the "conversational junkyard." She often sits at the kids' end or spends a great deal of time in the kitchen.

Furthermore, she may eagerly await the return of her spouse from work in order to catch up on news from the working world and share her news from the homefront, only to have her tired husband ready for some quiet time.

The "Shoptalk" of At-Home Motherhood May Not Seem Interesting to You

Mary, mother of three small sons, expressed her concern about having nothing interesting to say. "I guess when all day you deal with grime, green beans, and garbage bags, pretty soon your mind is filled with the same. It's pretty scary."

Although green beans and garbage bags are definitely part of the new vocabulary (instead of green beans, I always think of Cheerios and raisins—stuck in the carpet of course), they are only a small part of the shoptalk of at-home motherhood. You've got a lot more on your mind than that.

First of all, you think about bodily functions—feeding, handling bodily waste issues, nursing sick bodies back to health, tending to sanitary conditions in the home, regulating body temperatures with clothing. You deal with squirming, moist little bodies—life at its most basic level.

Second, you think about activities which, to the casual observer, might appear frivolous and merely decorative— buying new bathroom curtains, making a dried flower wreath, or arranging a beautiful bouquet of flowers. Yes, they are commonplace, "feminine," small acts in the grand scheme of things, but their effects are cumulative. They all contribute to creating a happy home, one that operates as a refuge from the unrelieved seriousness of the outside world.

And finally, you think about how to develop the strengths and resources of people in the family and community. Giving moral support, letting others let off steam, nursing bruised egos, coaching others to control impulsive actions—all are skills useful both at home and on the job to encourage those we care about.

Although the casual mindset of home, the lack of adult feedback, and the unsophisticated activities of childrearing can make the home-based mother feel that her mental life is becoming too one-dimensional, there is no need to panic. Research absolutely does not support fears that intelligence or verbal abilities decline because of staying at home full-time. But worrying about it is normal and healthy. It's healthy because a little discontent can motivate you to challenge yourself to grow during this period. The rest of this chapter offers suggestions for using your time at home as an opportunity for mental growth. You won't want to do everything, but do what you can. Your mind is worth it!

Be a Keen Observer of Human Nature

It takes time to develop insights about family and friends; therefore, the woman at home is in a unique position to cultivate her people powers. She can observe others to gain understanding about how people think and what motivates them. Charlene, a forty-one-year-old Saratoga housewife, tells the following story to illustrate this point.

She and her husband, Doug, go to the Christmas party for his software company. Over hors d'oeuvres she chats with the new vice-president, touted as the man who will turn the troubled company around. Charlene learns that he's renting a condo here while his wife stays in the "big house" in Boston. He is charming, but there is something about him that she instinctively mistrusts. Later she says to Doug, "You know the new VP who's supposed to do great things for the price of our stock? Well, I think he's through the revolving door. He's in for what he can get, then he's out."

It came as no surprise to Charlene that by the time the company picnic rolled around in July, the new man had moved back to Boston—through the revolving door.

How did Charlene know?

First of all, she asks different, more personal questions.

Second, she's not that interested in his resume, whereas Doug and many of his colleagues are so impressed with the

VP's achievements, they look no further than this impressive record.

Third, her finely-tuned antennae, trained at home to read people, easily picked up what he's really all about. Charlene's style of attentive listening beyond just the subject being discussed, a skill often associated with psychotherapy, is a powerful tool many women at home develop.

Schedule in Some "Mind Time"

Make a little time during these busy years to read, act, tutor, attend lectures, take courses, or do anything you find reawakens and stimulates your mind and soul. Some women report that they limit the time they spend on hands-on housewife/mothering activities to a flexible eight-hour workday. They wouldn't be caught dead folding laundry during naptime! Don't feel guilty about getting a sitter in order to buy some time—you're worth it.

"You Are What You Read"

This library bookmark's claim is good news for the housebound mother of small children. By reading you can traverse centuries and continents, explore fresh ideas and subtle insights, and you don't have to hire a sitter or pay for plane fare. When you're making up your reading list, don't stick to knitting. Make it a habit to branch out. Read about anything and everything that interests you.

✔ Read about architecture (Tom Wolf, *From Bauhaus to Our House* [New York: Farrar, Straus, Giroux, 1981]), computers (Tracy Kidder, *Soul of a New Machine* [Thorndike, Maine: Thorndike Press, 1981]), philosophy (Robert Pirsig, *Zen and the Art of Motorcycle Maintenance* [New York:

Morrow, 1974]), science (Carl Sagan, *Cosmos* [New York: Random House, 1980]), or business (Thomas Watson, Jr., *Father, Son and Co.*, [New York: Bantam, 1990]).

✔ Read a classic. Especially read one if you're having doubts about your decision to stay home full time. Remember, almost all classical literature—from the Bible to Homer to Joyce—features women who are not employed outside the home. Try George Eliot's *Middlemarch*, Jane Austen's *Pride and Prejudice*, D. H. Lawrence's *Sons and Lovers*, Steinbeck's *East of Eden*, or E. M. Forster's *Howard's End*.

✔ Read news, business, and financial magazines. Reading what's going on in the working world will help you stay in touch. After reading an especially interesting article, try to summarize the main points.

Maintain Professional Ties

Stay in touch with your field by reading, taking courses in your field and having lunch regularly with your colleagues. You never know when you might want to jump back in! If you see an article that might interest a former colleague, clip it and send it to him/her with a note.

Sign Up!

Joining a special interest group not only gives you a forum where you can share ideas and experiences, it also gets you out of the house. Keep in mind that it's acceptable to put volunteer activities on a resume, so when you sign up for a job, pick something that will develop your intellectual skills. For example, if you're going to be involved with your son's soccer league, sign up to be the publicity person rather than the one who brings Kool-Aid. Or if you want to get involved with your daughter's school, work on the PTA newsletter instead of the carpool. When you're at meetings, make it a point to participate in the discussions instead of hanging back.

Write

Keep a journal of your feelings, thoughts, impressions, favorite jokes or anecdotes, or well-turned phrases. If you write it down, you more than double your chances of recalling it later.

Discipline Your Mind

Force yourself to make your points logically and clearly. If you're discussing a third party (detractors call this gossip), tell a good story. When discussing a movie you've seen recently, practice telling the plot in some logical fashion instead of jumping around.

When you hear a word you don't understand, ask or look it up. Foreign phrases and acronyms needn't remain mysteries. When reading the paper or a magazine, read analytically. Try to wrap your mind around the issue so you understand clearly and with precision what it's all about.

Tune In to Stimulating Radio or Television Shows

Try the local CBS news station, with Charles Osgood's news shorts (retell them at dinner), or the local talk show station. For some solid intellectual input, try National Public

160

Radio and "All Things Considered," "Fresh Air," or anything Bill Moyers does.

Get Out with Adults As Much As Possible

Once a week get a sitter so that you and your spouse can go out. Skip the movies and head for a quiet restaurant where you can sip some Chardonnay and talk, talk, talk.

Keep Your Perspective Positive

Look at staying home full-time as being like a college education. At home you can learn skills and enhance relationships that will be important for the rest of your life. Don't worry about your mind turning to mush: You now have time to fill it with what you choose.

Exercises for Stimulating Your Mind

1. From the following list, check the qualities that describe you.

   ☐ good with numbers
   ☐ interested in learning
   ☐ fast on my feet
   ☐ curious about life
   ☐ up on current events
   ☐ good observer
   ☐ articulate
   ☐ logical
   ☐ analytical

- ☐ intuitive
- ☐ creative
- ☐ artistic
- ☐ witty
- ☐ intelligent

I like to:

- ☐ play word games
- ☐ work puzzles
- ☐ solve problems
- ☐ debate
- ☐ play the devil's advocate
- ☐ make puns
- ☐ speak publicly
- ☐ read
- ☐ play bridge
- ☐ write
- ☐ play memory games

What intellectual qualities does it take to succeed in these areas? For example, playing bridge requires, among other things, concentration and memory. You've now identified significant intellectual qualities in yourself.

2. List three intellectual areas which you would like to develop. Then, write down three ideas for developing each of these three areas.

3. What are three ways you could build more "mind time" into your schedule?

4. Make a reading list of at least ten books (fiction and non-fiction). As you read a book on the list, check it off. Peruse the book review section of your local paper (often on Sunday) for new additions.

5. List three radio or TV shows that you don't currently watch that would interest you and provide some good intellectual input. What times are they on? What chores could you plan to do that would allow you to watch or listen?

6. Who's your favorite columnist? Ellen Goodman, Anna Quindlen, George Will, Dave Barry? If you don't have one, follow the columns for a couple of weeks and pick one. Having a favorite will encourage you to follow his/her work carefully.

7. List three issues you feel strongly about (e.g., abortion, affirmative action, government defense spending). Now develop three logical arguments supporting your opinions. Watch the media for facts, stories, and incidents to add to your argument.

8. Think about what clubs, volunteer organizations, or classes you might like to sign up for. Write them all down. Now pick the top three. What phone calls would you need to make to get additional information? Put these phone calls on your "To Do" list for this week.

9. Think of three areas for study you always thought *might* interest you but that you never pursued (e.g., art, psychology, history).

10. What steps could you take to learn something about these areas?

12

"Let's Get Physical"

In my personal dream...families would exercise
together, share their daily progress in moving toward
individual health goals, and feel free to share their
problems and release their tensions and stresses in a
constructive, healing way in one another's presence.
— Kenneth Cooper, describing his concept
of the "aerobic family"[1]

Let's face it: we need to keep our strength up. Our job
demands the physical stamina of a hod carrier. The ethereal,
fragile Madonna of baby formula commercials, cradling her
infant tenderly in her ultra-slim arms, clearly does not have the
upper body strength for the real job. Anyone who has lifted,
toted, chased, or cleaned up after the average toddler can tell
you that fitness is no frill. It is a job requirement.

We are also role models for our children. If we want them
to lead healthy, active lives and make the most of who they are,
we had better do the same. Now is the right time to make eating
right and physical fitness a priority. With a little extra effort

---

[1] *Aerobics Program* 199.

and planning, we're in a prime position to start living the healthiest lifestyle ever.

This chapter is not about magical grapefruit and banana diets. Nor will it recommend Saran body wraps to rid you of cellulite, stretch marks and extra fat cells. This chapter is not about swimming the Nile or running a five-minute mile. It promotes an active lifestyle—not necessarily an athletic one. It cannot promise a transformation into a whole new you. Your metamorphosis into an at-home mother—a butterfly emerging from the chrysalis—is enough of a transformation. Yes, in my book you are a butterfly—you only feel like you're turning into a caterpillar. Therefore, we will lightly touch on habits and routines that will make you feel as beautiful as you really are.

The tips in this chapter offer some positive diet, exercise, and grooming options available to you and your family. We will focus on the following:

- ✔ how to cook and eat light and healthy foods
- ✔ exercise routines that fit your busy lifestyle
- ✔ the joys of sharing an active lifestyle with your family
- ✔ the importance of maintaining personal grooming routines

We Are What We Eat

The way we feel depends, to a much greater degree than most of us realize, on the way we eat. Yet we sometimes seem to expect that our bodies can take anything we put in them and produce good results. Not so. Food can make us feel full, obese, bloated, headachy, and enervated, not to mention sick. Conversely, food can make us feel trim and fit, inspired, vital, happy and healthy, full of energy.

Often the head dieticians and cooks in our homes, at-home mothers need to be aware of those foods that make the body run smoothly and those that cause breakdowns in the body's systems. Keeping up with nutritional breakthroughs—and separating sense from nonsense—is a tall order but well worth the effort. Toward this end I suggest you start a collection of cookbooks based on the most current nutritional knowledge. The Cooking Light series (Birmingham, Alabama: Oxmoor House, Inc., 1986), for example, specializes in low-fat recipes that will help you plan meals rich in nutrients without sacrificing one iota in taste or texture.

Here are some recent medical facts that have changed the way we look at food:

✔ If we reduce our consumption of fat, salt, and cholesterol, we also reduce our risk of heart disease and other degenerative diseases such as high blood pressure, gout, and even certain cancers.

✔ High cholesterol levels, one of the leading causes of heart disease, can be significantly lowered by reducing the amount of saturated fat in our diet and by limiting our consumption of egg yolks and whole-milk dairy products.

✔ We can reduce our risk of osteoporosis, a disease commonly afflicting post-menopausal women that leaves the bones brittle and porous, by taking in calcium through low-fat dairy products.

✔ Eating dietary fiber found in unrefined carbohydrates such as fresh fruits and vegetables and in whole grain versions of bread, cereal and pasta, brown rice, dried beans, nuts, and seeds can reduce our risk of intestinal disorders and certain forms of cancer.

In order to eat more healthily, many of us need to reformulate the balance of food categories found in our diets. Most of the food we eat is in one of three forms: protein, carbohydrates (unrefined and refined) and fats. A commonly recommended proportion is fifteen percent protein, sixty to sixty-five percent carbohydrates, and twenty to twenty-five percent fats.

We need very little fat in our diets: a large bowl of oatmeal covers the requirement. Some people put more butter on a single morning's toast than their bodies need for an entire week! Many of us also eat more protein than our bodies can handle because we have the false impression that protein is the food that gives us the most energy and strength. We think nothing of sitting down to a ten-ounce steak after having consumed a hamburger for lunch. The recommended serving of protein is only 3½ ounces (about the size of a deck of cards)!

We need more unrefined carbohydrates, that is, starches and sugars in their natural state. In their original state, these foods are nutritionally balanced, providing ample carbohydrates, protein, fat, vitamins, and minerals. They are high in fiber, not in calories. Unrefined carbohydrates are the body's most efficient fuel. However, through refining and processing, these foods lose their nutritional value. Stripped of their low-calorie, bulk-providing fiber, what's left is unbalanced nutritionally, depleted of vitamins and minerals, and fattening. A given volume of food in its natural state contains fewer calories and more bulk than the same food that has been processed. For example, a whole orange (thirty-nine calories) equals only one third of a cup of juice after the bulk of the orange has been removed, but the juice still has the same calories. Refined carbohydrates—cakes, candy, ice cream, chips, cookies, white bread, pastry—are our dietary nemesis. They offer a very sluggish fuel for our bodies, cause weight gain, and, some believe, can cause us to become hyper, crashing later in a sugar low.

What follow are some ideas for healthy cooking and eating that are aimed at a diet high in minerals, vitamins and fiber and low in fat, sugar, and salt. By incorporating "on the lighter side" eating habits, we should be able to eat to our satisfaction without gaining weight. Often, just by eliminating empty foods from our diet and making the calories we eat count, we will naturally and slowly shed extra pounds.

Eating and Cooking for Health

Purge Your Pantry of Junk Foods—Permanently

Restock with light, nutritious ingredients, using the following guidelines.

- ✔ Buy whole-grain cereals, both brown and enriched long-grain white rice, whole grain breads rather than cottony white loaves, and, of course, lots of fresh fruits.

- ✔ Buy skim and low-fat milk, yogurt, and cheeses for rich sources of calcium! Check with your pediatrician to see what type of milk he or she recommends for children.

- ✔ Stock bouillon granules. They are lower in fat and sodium (salt) than most canned broths or cubes.

- ✔ If the only vegetables you're eating are the pickles on your hamburgers, veg out at the supermarket. Try acorn squash, Brussels sprouts, leeks, kohlrabi, artichokes, eggplant, bean sprouts, different types of squash, collard and turnip greens, red, yellow and green peppers, and carrots.

- ✔ Use margarine instead of butter. It's just as caloric as butter, but it's healthier because it's made with unsaturated fat. Cut back on the amount of margarine in recipes by a third.

- ✔ Use vegetable oil, preferably sunflower, safflower, or olive oil.

- ✔ Buy vegetable cooking spray and use it instead of butter or oil; also use it to coat baking sheets, casseroles, or muffin tins.

Tips for Healthy Cooking

Now that you're stocked with the right stuff, try some of these cooking ideas.

✔ Cut fats from your diet by adding more poultry and fish and reducing beef, lamb and pork.

✔ Try stir-frying instead of deep-frying, steaming instead of boiling, or rack-roasting instead of cooking in greasy drippings. Meats, fish, and chicken will taste tender and juicy without rich sauces; vegetables retain their color and crunch.

✔ Remember that the shorter the cooking time for fruits and vegetables, the fewer nutrients you will lose.

✔ Trim all fat and remove skin from poultry either before cooking or before serving.

✔ Make hearty homemade vegetable and grain soups instead of creamed and canned soups.

✔ Use cornstarch instead of cream, butter, or flour to thicken a sauce. Use half as much cornstarch as you would flour.

✔ Use beans and peas in recipes. They are an inexpensive source of vegetable protein and fiber and they don't contain fat or cholesterol.

✔ Defat soups, stews, and gravies by making them ahead of time and refrigerating them. When the fat congeals, you can easily remove it.

✔ Remove salt and oil from canned vegetables and tuna by rinsing before cooking, or buy water-packed tuna.

✔ Flavor your food with a variety of herbs and spices. Chives, dill, sesame seed, rosemary and tarragon are good with most vegetables, while onion, thyme, sage, rosemary, and oregano can perk up meats, fish and poultry. Of course, parsley and garlic go with practically everything!

✔ Flavor with wine: the rich flavor remains after the alcohol and calories evaporate.

✔ Build up a repertoire of good tomato- and olive oil-based pasta sauce recipes. Keep mushrooms, capers, black olives, eggplant, peppers and pine nuts handy to throw in the sauce. Top with low-fat Parmesan or Romano cheese.

✔ Make interesting salads. Go for color with carrot shavings, some red cabbage, last night's vegetables, rice and pasta. Use low-fat salad dressings made from scratch.

✔ Don't forget the much-maligned baked potato, a rich source of nutrients, especially if you eat the peel. It has the same number of calories as an apple, unless it is loaded with fattening toppings.

✔ Drink several glasses of water a day. Nothing helps your complexion and keeps those cells plump and young like lots of drinking water!

✔ Pay attention to what you and your family members eat. You might be surprised at how much food with zilch nutritional value we pop into our mouths.

✔ Don't skip meals. In addition to decreasing your blood sugar level and making you irritable, missing a meal only serves to make you hungrier for the next one and more likely to overeat junk foods.

If you eat a balanced diet, assuming you eat regular portions, you will have no problems maintaining your weight.

Usually, just by eating healthily and by exercising, extra weight will slowly disappear. However, if you want to lose a significant amount of weight, more than ten pounds or so, you can do so by paying special attention to your diet. You can lose weight without feeling hungry or deprived just by tipping your eating patterns in favor of those foods that will help you lose pounds.

Exercise for Fitness

To achieve fitness, we need to partner good eating habits with exercise. The benefits of exercise are well-known: a slimmer, firmer body, vitality and zest, better health and a longer life, mental alertness, reduced stress level, sounder sleep. Still need convincing? Consider this: If, over the period of a year, we eat just one hundred excess calories per day (the caloric content of a plain doughnut), we gain an extra ten pounds. Unchecked, that ten pounds translates into a walloping fifty pounds in five years! However, a brisk half-hour walk each day will offset that gain. I can't think of any more worthwhile home project, can you?

In spite of knowing exercise is good for us, we find ways to resist "taking the medicine." The fleets of stationary bicycles gathering dust and the piles of unused health club memberships across the land attest to the difficulty we have getting motivated to exercise—and staying motivated.

"I'm too tired from cleaning the house stem to stern."

"I already get enough exercise chasing the kids around. Besides, who will watch the kids while I go out for a walk?"

"The sun will give me skin cancer."

"I don't own a Lycra or Spandex anything."

"I can't afford a health club."

"My body's hopeless—why bother?"

"Maybe someday, but not right now."

The law of inertia dictates that it's much easier to sit around in tight clothes making excuses than it is to get up and move our bodies. Certainly no one will give us the extra time. Our families will never tell us they don't need us for a couple of hours. They always need us! But time is available if exercise is a priority.

This section outlines a three-point exercise program that includes:

✔ following an exercise routine that develops flexibility, overall strength and cardiovascular fitness

✔ leading an active lifestyle throughout the day

✔ making fitness a family affair

The goal? No, it's not to fit into a Perfect Size 8. The goal is simply to make exercise a habit that becomes a regular part of your life.

Choose the Right Exercise Routine for You

The right exercise routine for you is one that you enjoy. Let me put it another way: If you don't get some enjoyment from it, you won't stick to it. Ideally, your routine will integrate exercises for cardiovascular fitness (aerobic exercise), flexibility, and muscle strength. The standard good advice from experts is to perform an aerobic activity—one that places great demands on the body so that the cardiovascular system is forced to improve its capacity to handle oxygen—for twenty to sixty minutes, three to five times a week, plus doing muscle strengthening and stretching exercises. Some good aerobic exercises include brisk walking, running, swimming, biking, cross country skiing, jumping rope, rowing, singles tennis, racquetball, squash, handball, and aerobic dance.

Stretching before aerobic exercise results in a supple, more flexible body that can move through a workout with greater ease and grace. A body with the "kinks" worked out is also less likely to get injured and less likely to develop back problems.

Supplemental exercises for strength such as curl-ups and push-ups or modified versions thereof are also important.

Strong muscles not only help us achieve good posture, thereby decreasing the risk of low-back pain, but they help us perform daily tasks that involve lifting, pulling, or pushing objects. "In an emergency," says the American Alliance of Health, Physical Education, Recreation and Dance (AAHPERD), "the ability to apply force with the upper body can mean the difference between a serious injury and escaping harm."[2]

Here are some points to keep in mind as you begin your exercise program:

- ✔ Check with your doctor if you've just had a baby, if you have a history of heart trouble or other chronic health problem, or are more than twenty percent overweight.

- ✔ Don't set yourself up for being an exercise dropout by setting unrealistic goals. For those of us with babies, for example, regular brisk strolls with the baby and vigorous gardening is a good starting routine.

- ✔ If you work out alone, check out records, videos, or books from the public library to find a routine that you like; if you prefer company, try to find a friend in the neighborhood with children close in age to yours and get together to workout. Or sign up for an exercise class at a local workout facility, YMCA, school or community center. Whatever you do, do it regularly.

- ✔ Vary your menu of exercise. As soon as one becomes a chore, try something else. My current (it changes regularly due to my and my family's schedules) routine is this eclectic one: Three times a week or more I do some sort of aerobic activity. Usually I take a fast hour-long

---

[2] Quoted in Glover and Shepherd 23.

walk with Elizabeth in her stroller, who happily munches on the snacks I've prepared so she won't want to stop constantly; then I log in one or two twenty-five-minute runs around the neighborhood; finally, on the weekend, some friends and I go on a "butt-burner" hill walk. I stretch before I leave the house or out in front of my friend's house while I wait for her to emerge. While Elizabeth is splashing in the tub, I sandwich in some more stretching and "old-lady" (my daughters' term) sit-ups and push-ups. I'm definitely not working all my muscle groups, but it will have to do for now. I also enjoy trying out other people's workouts. When I was in Houston visiting my brother's family, my sister-in-law introduced me to Step Aerobics—and to some previously undiscovered groups of muscles in my calves! If you let people know you're into exercise, they will usually love to share their own fitness tips and routines.

✔ Learn how to do stretches and exercises correctly. Many of the things you learned back in high school were wrong and can injure your back.

Adopt an Active Lifestyle

Leading an active lifestyle means being active throughout the day, not just during your twenty-minute workout. By trying to keep our bodies in motion as much as possible, we fight the sedentary syndrome that finds us supine in front of the tube with a bowl of high-fat, high-sugar snack, exercising by raising our hands to the mouth in a steady motion. It means we stop trying to park in the closest spot; it means we never take an elevator less than three flights (when we're without small children); it means we walk our kids to school, to the store, or to a friend's house. It means saying, "Sure, why not!" when a friend suggests an outing. It means not saying, "I'm busy," when our five year old wants help learning to ride his two-wheeler.

By cultivating a pro-active attitude, we find hidden workouts in our daily chores like sweeping the walk, raking leaves or washing windows. By welcoming rather than dreading opportunities to reach, bend, twist and lift, we strengthen little-used muscles and move our bodies the way they were designed to move. In this way, moving, one of life's necessities, also becomes one of life's joys.

Make Fitness a Family Affair

Don't let fitness pass your children by. According to Bob Glover and Jack Shepherd, leading experts in the field of fitness, in their book *The Family Fitness Handbook*, our children are "dangerously out of shape and unable to carry on their daily work or physically demanding recreational activities" (5). Often unfit and frequently overweight, our kids, say Glover and Shepherd, are in worse shape than kids were ten years ago, and this is endangering their health.

As parents, we play the key role in keeping our children in shape and able to carry on their daily activities with vigor. Not only can we serve as fitness role models as they observe us leading an active lifestyle, but we can also commit ourselves to exercising with them. By being involved with them in exercise, we can teach them that health and fitness can be fun. Then they'll be more likely to have healthy exercise habits as adults.

Here are five tips adapted from *The Family Fitness Handbook* that will help you work the "Three Fs"—Fun, Fellowship, and Fitness—into your family life.

✔ Relearn how to "come out and play."
Unstructured spontaneity—in other words,
play—may take some practice for us rules- and
task-oriented adults. Go with the flow. Kids

love family exercise if it's presented as a game and it's done at their own speed. Don't worry about sticking to one activity. Kids under the age of six can't possibly concentrate on one activity for too long. Play catch for a while, then swing, act like a monkey, throw a Frisbee around, play freeze tag. Anything that looks like exercise to you—but looks like a game to them—will do.

✔ Involve your children in your own workouts. Let them stretch with you or ride their bicycles alongside you when you run. When you go biking, let an older child accompany you. Introduce a younger child to the joys of biking by having her sit in a bike seat (wearing her own helmet), or better yet, in a bike trailer. Let your kids dance along with your video workout.

✔ Consider a family gift of a membership to a fitness club where the whole family can swim, play tennis, or work out together.

✔ Schedule weekly or monthly fitness activities. Sign up for a community family fun run or walk; take walks with a special destination in mind, like a pond to see the ducks or a store where the kids can buy candy (sugarless, of course!). Plan a bicycle trip in the countryside or a hiking expedition in a national forest. Regardless of the activity, always take plenty of breaks and lots of healthy snacks!

✔ Do yourself and your kids a favor by limiting the amount of time they spend in front of the TV. The two to four hours of viewing could be spent in more active and productive play, including exercise.

Keeping Up Appearances

The real reason to exercise and eat healthy foods is to feel better, but the truth of the matter is that most women are motivated to eat right and exercise in order to look good. The sense of well-being that comes from taking pride in one's appearance and from leading a healthy lifestyle are particularly crucial at this critical juncture in our lives, in which all sorts of mixed messages about our physical appearance intersect: feelings of shaky vanity and the fear of losing our looks clash with feelings of maternal pride and contentment and the feminist belief that however we look should be good enough.

One of the nice things about maturing is accepting certain truths about yourself, doing what works for you, and liberating yourself from "shoulds" and "shouldn'ts." If you are happy as a clam in your jeans and sweats and staying home means never (well, hardly ever) having to worry about matched accessories or make-up again, don't read the rest of this chapter. Others feel better when they pamper themselves with beauty routines.

We know that if we "dress for success" for a job interview, we enhance our chances of getting the job. The same psychological principle applies at home. Putting a little extra time into our appearance—carefully applied make-up (if make-up is part of your regular image), clean, styled hair, a nice outfit— can give our self-confidence a boost so that we feel ready to face whatever the day brings. By establishing regular beauty routines, when the doorbell rings unexpectedly at two P.M., we won't be tempted to hide behind the front door. We won't have to pretend that nobody's home because we still haven't updated the cave-dweller look resulting from last night's interrupted sleep.

Setting aside the time to fix our hair and make-up isn't always easy with small children underfoot, but once done, it goes a long way toward making our days go more smoothly. Some women prefer to shower, fix their hair and make-up and dress for the day early in the morning before they dress the kids. Others wait until they finish some of the sweatier details of housework, yardwork and exercise before they undertake their own self-beautification project. Still others get ready to face the world in stages. They squeeze in a shower before their husband leaves for work, dry their hair when the kids are planted in front of Barney, wear rollers while they vacuum, and applying make-up during naptime. Both early and late bloomers usually do some early evening "reclamation work" to freshen up before dinner. The exact timing doesn't matter; what does matter is that you get whatever makes you feel good done at some point every day.

Here are some beautiful ideas for at-home maintenance:

✔ Like the song says, everybody's beautiful, in her own way, so think positively when you look into the mirror. Stand up straight and tighten your abdominals: this forces you, like an airplane seat, into an upright position—and into a more positive attitude. Try a little of the unabashed admiration that your toddler uses when he looks at himself in the mirror. Do not be preoccupied with your flaws. If you find yourself focusing on a poochy stomach, veined legs, too large nose, whatever, practice saying to yourself, "So what!" Chances are, you're exaggerating the flaws anyway. Studies show that women negatively distort what they see. They think they are heavier and more wrinkled than they really are. Interestingly, our male counterparts distort in the positive direction. Who says we have nothing to learn from men?

✔ Find a flattering hairstyle, then maintain it. Now is not the time to start cutting or coloring your own hair unless you receive some guidance from a knowledgeable source. One bad amateur color job and your self-image along with your orange, broken-off hair will take a beating for months.

✔ Spend a little time planning your outfit. Get rid of the ratty garments from your closet so that you're not tempted to wear them.

✔ For those who quit a career to come home, occasionally wear some of your great work clothes that are now gathering dust on their hangers. Besides giving you a lift, you'll be getting some use from clothes that may well be out of style by the time you go back to work.

✔ Don't abandon the little self-pampering luxuries you enjoyed before you had kids. If you're so inclined, enjoy the luxury of a European spa in your own home. Put your husband in charge of the real world while you take time out for a bubble bath. Then give yourself a manicure and a pedicure, tweeze your eyebrows, and condition your hair. Treat yourself to a facial mask. Put wet teabags over your eyes to remove puffiness. If you don't have time to keep your nails polished, either keep them filed and natural or go acrylic. Acrylic nails are relatively cheap and they wear like iron. They're perfect for removing "scratch and sniff" stickers from walls and cabinets!

✔ Invite a friend over for a home spa event and give each other a make-over. Focus the conversation on the fine art of body maintenance. Solicit feedback on a potential new hairdo or make-up approach; try out each other's lipstick and swap make-up and hair tips. These grooming sessions still serve a social purpose that didn't end with adolescent slumber parties!

✔ If you're the type who loves to keep up with
   fashion trends, read women's magazines for
   new hair and make-up techniques and fashion
   ideas. Warning: Reading fashion magazines
   may be hazardous to your self-esteem. Research
   indicates that after reading fashion magazines
   featuring gorgeous models with perfect faces
   and bodies (Is there any other kind?), women
   feel more dissatisfied with their own bodies and
   faces. Therefore, read fashion magazines with
   caution. Make sure you only come away with
   new ideas and techniques; leave the idealized
   standards of perfection for the recycle bin.
   Remember the words of Abe Lincoln upon
   overhearing someone remark that he was a
   "common-looking man": "Friend, the Lord
   prefers common-looking people. That is the
   reason he makes so many of them."

Mark Twain once said that you can't throw a habit out the
window. You have to coax it down the stairs one step at a time.
With work and determination, you can coax yourself and your
family into developing good eating and exercise habits. This
takes time—not surprising considering the long years it takes
for a body's health to deteriorate or its shape to bulge and sag.
So push your fitness program and keep pushing it. Together
as a family, discuss personal grooming, nutrition, exercise, and
weight management. By making fitness and health a priority
in your home, you will truly give your family a gift that will
last a lifetime.

Exercises for Helping You Stay Healthy

Appearance

1. How much time do you spend every day on personal grooming? Describe your grooming routine.

2. What activities related to grooming do you do on a weekly basis? Monthly? Other?

3. Are you satisfied with your beauty routine? Are you satisfied with the results? If not, why not? What changes could you make to improve your beauty routine? List at least three.

4. What are your beauty strengths (ask friends or relatives if you can't think of enough)? List at least three.

5. Which of your physical characteristics would you like to improve? Make sure you pick something that can be changed on your own and not with the help of cosmetic surgery.

Nutrition

1. Describe your level of nutrition knowledge.
   - ☐ Very knowledgeable
   - ☐ Above average knowledge
   - ☐ Average knowledge
   - ☐ Very little knowledge

2. Do you eat healthy food?
   - ☐ Always
   - ☐ Most of the time
   - ☐ Sometimes
   - ☐ Seldom

3. Does your family eat healthy food?

☐ Always

☐ Most of the time

☐ Sometimes

☐ Seldom

4. What changes in your eating habits reflect new knowledge in the field of medicine and nutrition?

5. What cookbooks or books on nutrition do you use as resources?

6. List at least three steps you could take to improve the nutritional quality of the foods you and your family eat.

7. In your view, what are your weaknesses in terms of eating healthy foods?

Fitness

1. Are you already at the weight you want to be? If not, what changes could you make in your current diet that would allow you to lose weight slowly and painlessly over the next year? List three.

2. Are you physically fit?

☐ Very fit

☐ Above average fitness

☐ Average fitness

☐ Below average fitness

☐ Not at all fit

3. Do friends and relatives often hint that you need to get out and get some exercise? Do you catch yourself saying to yourself all the time, "I've got to start exercising!"?

4. How much time every week do you spend exercising? Describe your workout. What other forms of exercise do you get?

5. Do you want to workout more? If so, what reasons do you usually give to yourself for not doing it? What strategies could you use to overcome your objections?

6. What forms of aerobic exercise do you enjoy?

7. Do you stretch before working out? Describe your stretching routine.

8. Do you do exercises for muscle strength? Which muscles do you concentrate on?

9. Do you prefer to exercise alone or with company? What exercise classes in your area would you like to sign up for?

10. How much time do you spend in front of the TV? How much time do your children spend in front of the TV? Be honest.

11. What steps could you take to start leading a more active lifestyle? List at least three.

12. Do your children see you as a positive fitness role model? If yes, in what ways? If not, what can you do to remedy the situation?

13. Do you ever exercise with your children? List three exercises you could share with your children.

14. In what family fitness activities have you participated in the last year? What activities could you plan for the coming year that your whole family would enjoy?

13

Practicing Assertiveness

"Can I borrow your camcorder when we're on
vacation?"
"Mom, could you bake two dozen cookies for tomorrow
morning?"
"Can you watch Lindsay for me this afternoon?"
"Would you be willing to head up the committee again
next year?"

— Four opportunities to be assertive

If we lack assertiveness skills, common requests like these can steal our peace of mind and tie up our stomachs in knots of anxiety. Our families, friends and even total strangers can rob us of the energy and time we need to devote to our own priorities. However, by developing the ability to express our views honestly and directly without hurting others—the essence of assertiveness—we can control what goes on in our own backyards and in our lives. Whether we choose to work on math facts or puzzles, to fly kites or build sandcastles, to design a gazebo or learn how to raise bees, assertiveness skills back up our choices.

Most women are incredibly tuned in to others' needs, wishes, feelings, and rights. Why, then, do we find it so difficult to express our own needs and wishes? As we strive to be good mothers and wives, we often try to do everything for everybody all the time. Why, then, do we feel uncomfortable asking others to do for us? We are often buffeted about on the high seas of infantile rage, temper tantrums, crying jags, and outrageous demands by our small children, who, it seems, were born assertive. Why, then, do we feel so anxious at the prospect of a negative encounter with a rational adult? Furthermore, why does a woman with a reputation for being a tough customer on the job turn into a "mouseburger"—Helen Gurley Brown's term for an unassertive woman—once she's at home with her husband and family?

Although the reasons why a woman doesn't speak up for herself are as complex and individual as each woman's thumbprint, some common patterns do emerge. She may have been brought up in the "think it but don't say it" school. Often this same school of thought has socialized girls to believe that as mothers they must always put their husbands and children first. But fear is the most pervasive reason for denying ourselves: fear of making our family and friends angry with us if we refuse their requests; fear of being considered pushy or selfish or obnoxious or greedy; fear that if we rock the boat instead of just rocking the cradle, we threaten the security of the relationships on which we depend.

The problem is, when we ignore our own feelings and rights, always deferring to others, we begin to think of ourselves as second-class citizens. Playing doormat virtually invites others to use us to wipe their feet. Then we either become martyred and downtrodden or we become angry and resentful underneath the surface, furious at others for using us but feeling powerless to change the situation. These pent-up resentments may explode later in inappropriate outbursts. Either way, we risk driving away or losing the respect of those whose love and respect we want the most. Assertive behavior prevents all of this.

What Assertiveness Is and Is Not

In general people behave in one of four ways in a given situation:

✔ *Passive* behavior is classic "doormat" behavior: self-sacrificing, inhibited, fearful, helpless. When we behave passively, we allow others to make decisions and then resent it. When we behave passively, we expect sympathy and rewards for always giving way, but rarely get it.

✔ When we are *indirectly aggressive,* we use flattery, manipulation or trickery. We aim at getting our own way or at punishing others without honestly confronting a problem. The "silent treatment" is an example of indirect aggression.

✔ When we are *aggressive,* we use angry outbursts, bullying and belittling to enforce our will and seek to demean and humiliate others. The message? I'm OK. You are not.

✔ *Assertive* behavior is the ideal response. When we are assertive, we express our views honestly, openly, spontaneously, all the while respecting the rights and feelings of other people. When we behave assertively, we don't evade difficult situations that need to be cleared up. Our assertive behavior won't always get us what we want, but sometimes just the fact that we have expressed ourselves and been acknowledged makes "winning" seem less important. Furthermore, assertiveness is the only behavior pattern that makes win-win solutions possible. Assertive behavior involves being aware of what you want and knowing a few communication techniques.

Assertiveness is not an excuse to worm out of our legitimate responsibilities. Being assertive is also not being pushy or giving orders or getting your way all the time. And it's also not a license to open your mouth and fire any time you feel like it—that's aggression.

Let's take some situations common among at-home mothers that illustrate passive, indirect aggressive, aggressive, and assertive responses.

Scenario One

Barbara's long-lost college friend and her two small children are going to be in town for a week and would like to stay with her. She would like to spend some time with them, but the visit couldn't come at a more inconvenient time: her son is having tubes put in his ears and she has no spare room.

- ✔ Passive Response: "Well, I guess so...if you don't mind little James' crying and a messy house. Uh, what do your kids like to eat?" (She knocks herself out preparing fancy meals and sightseeing, spending way too much money and exhausting herself. She spends a miserable week being resentful and angry with herself for allowing them to impose on her at an inconvenient time; her husband is angry at her for letting them stay.)

- ✔ Indirect Aggressive Response: "Oh, it'll be so good to see you. Johnny's having surgery, but it will be fine." (When they arrive, she makes them feel unwelcome by disappearing for long periods of time and devoting herself to Johnny to the exclusion of everybody and everything else. By not saying "No" directly, the week and probably the friendship are both ruined.)

- ✔ Aggressive Response: "No way. It's impossible for us to have company right now!" (Her rather brusque rejection is unnecessary.)

✔ Assertive Response: "No, I'm really sorry, but it's not a good time. I would love to see you though—can you postpone your trip for a couple of weeks?" (She starts off with "No" so there can be no confusion; she states her position firmly and clearly without the need for extensive apologizing and beating around the bush.)

Scenario Two

Pat's friends call and invite her to go on a long walk. She would love to get out of the house for some exercise and social time, but she needs to bathe Jenny and put her to bed. Her husband is reading the paper.

✔ Passive Response: "No (*sighs deeply*), I couldn't possibly. I'm getting ready to give Jenny a bath. Unless John would...(*looks over at John, whose head is buried deep in the paper*). No, sorry. I've got too much to do." (Feels sorry for herself the rest of the night.)

✔ Indirect Aggressive Response: "I'd love to go but I've got to give Jenny her bath. John's probably too busy to help me" (*Looks over at John, who doesn't move.*) She repeats, this time more loudly, "John's probably too busy to help out." (Because she expects John to read her mind and because he can't, she gives him the silent treatment and slams around the kitchen. Eventually she explodes over something that has nothing to do with the real reason she's angry.)

✔ Aggressive Response: "Yes, John will just have to take over with the bath detail. He's only doing his usual couch potato routine." She throws the bath towel at him and says. "You're

on and I'm outta here." (Now he's angry at the
way she treated him.)

✔ Assertive Response: "John, I'd really like to go
on a walk with Anita and Debbie. It's been a
long day. Would you take over Jenny's bath
and read her a story?" (She states her request
directly, shows why it's important to her, and
also recognizes he has the right to refuse. She
doesn't attack his worth as a father.)

Scenario Three

Diane has headed up the big school fundraiser for two
years now and would really like to have this year off to take
some classes. The new PTA president, whom she respects and
admires, calls her and asks you if she'll do it again this year.

✔ Passive Response: "Well, I was kind of hoping
to have more time, but I guess if you can't find
anybody else." (Diane will be paying for her
mouseburger response for the rest of the year
and won't get started on her master's degree.)

✔ Indirect Aggressive Response: "Well, okay, I
guess I'll do it." (She proceeds to put no energy
into the job. She's late for meetings, doesn't turn
in reports, and continually complains about
how poorly organized the PTA is this year.)

✔ Aggressive Response: "Isn't it enough that I've
done it for two years? Why don't you try one of
the mothers who never do anything!" (Diane
alienates an influential community member.
Her reckless remarks show complete
insensitivity to the PTA president's legitimate
right to ask her to continue in the job.)

✔ Assertive Response: "I'm going to have to pass
it up this year as I've already committed myself
to going back to school. Good luck finding

someone." (Diane's response is direct and to the point; the PTA president will respect her straightforward reply so that she can get on with her staffing requirements.)

A "purely" aggressive or assertive or passive or indirectly aggressive person is rare. Depending on the situation, most of us behave in all four ways at various times. Some of us who are assertive with other women can seldom refuse requests from men. Other women can stand their own ground with everyone but their own children. As you read through this chapter, try to identify your trouble spots. Think about the areas where you are unassertive—at home, in groups, with strangers, with men, with your children, with friends, with your parents, and so on—and channel your efforts toward assertiveness in that direction.

This chapter focuses on some assertiveness skills that are frequently troublesome for at-home mothers: how to say "no," how to set limits, how to make requests, how to receive praise, how to give and receive criticism. It then presents some common scenarios for your practice of assertive behavior.

Saying "No"

Any at-home mother who wants to avoid feeling over-committed and frustrated will have to learn to say "no." Well-meaning husbands, friends, and children bombard us with demands on a daily basis. Some of these demands are appropriate, and even though we may prefer doing something else, we choose to say "yes." (Again, assertiveness is not a tool to be used to shirk responsibility.) However, other demands may be inappropriate and at times downright frivolous. Unfortunately, there are still many naive individuals who assume—unless you tell them otherwise—that you have nothing better to do because you don't work outside the home.

Perhaps you've tried the "putting a smile on your face and just saying yes" route only to find yourself complaining bitterly to friends about being exploited. Maybe you've tried the sulking and moping routine and found that doesn't work any better. If so, it's high time you cultivate the delicate art of saying "no."

Tips for Saying "No"

✔ The surprise element is often responsible for capturing a "yes" from you when you want to say "no." Try to anticipate situations so you can think through your assertive response in advance. However, when a request does take you by surprise, don't automatically say "yes." Instead, buy yourself some time by saying, "Let me think about it. I'll let you know as soon as I can" or "I need to discuss it with my family. I'll call you back tomorrow."

✔ Make sure you understand exactly what is being requested. Ask for clarification and for more information if you're not sure.

✔ Start your answer with the word "no" if that's what you want the outcome of the conversation to be. Without the definite "no," you'll end up saying "maybe" or "yes" and will have to revisit the problem later.

✔ Speak in a firm voice.

✔ Keep it short. If you start in with long, drawn-out excuses, apologies, rationalizations and explanations, you might end up giving in.

✔ Don't say "no" if there's a good reason to say "yes." Learning to say "no" is not meant to encourage selfishness or doing less than your fair share. Consider all the angles before giving your answer.

191

✔ Consider this bonus: Your skill at saying "no" won't be lost on your sons and daughters. With you as their model they will be more likely to keep from being pressured into sex, alcohol and other drugs when they become teenagers.

Practice Saying "No"

Assume that in the following scenarios you want to say "no." What would the assertive response be? How does that compare to what you would do in the real situation?

1. Your neighbor asks you to babysit her two children because she has a hair appointment and couldn't get a sitter. You frequently watch her children and know she tends to roll in a half-hour or so late. She calls you on a day you had set aside to catch up on bill paying and other paperwork. What do you do?

2. You're in line at the supermarket with a cart full of groceries. The express lane is closed. You just let one person go in front of you. Now another woman asks, "Can I go through?" What do you do?

3. You've volunteered to keep your friend's child over the weekend so that she and her husband can go to an out-of-town wedding. She calls you the day before and asks if you would make sure her daughter gets driven to her hair cut appointment and to and from soccer practice, and, since she stays late at school Friday afternoon for tutoring, she needs to be picked up instead of taking the bus. You already have too many other events to drive to. What do you say?

4. A friend stops by to visit. Her young child has a runny nose and is coughing. Your family vacation is coming up and you don't want to

take a chance that the kids come down with something before the trip. What do you do?

5. You've already signed up for two magazine subscriptions that you don't really want in an effort to support the Athletic Boosters at the local high school. You look out your window and see your neighbor's son heading to your front door with his magazine subscription sign-up packet. What do you do?

Setting Limits

Every morning Mary dresses her kids, prepares and cleans up their breakfast, packs their lunches, makes their beds and picks up their messes, touches up their bathroom, and drives them to a school well within walking distance. She often makes an extra trip to deliver forgotten lunches or homework assignments. All this between seven and nine A.M.! She really starts steppin' and fetchin' from three to nine in the afternoon!

Supermom or Superslave? Only Mary knows for sure. She alone can determine what she's willing to do for others and how she wants others to treat her. She alone can set limits.

We decide the limits in advance; our skill at saying "no" will enforce those limits. We also recognize that—like all limits—these are made to be broken once in a while. We decide how much time we need to do our own thing. We decide if we will accept phone calls at dinner or how long we want the phone lines to be tied up with children's calls, how much chauffeuring and errand-running we're willing to do, whether we're entitled to take a bath alone without kids trooping in asking questions. By setting limits, we encourage our children and others to be more independent and more self-sufficient.

Tips for Setting Limits

✔ Make sure you think through your standards so you can communicate the limits you are setting. Getting your standards clear in your head will help you make a more forceful case when saying "no." Let your kids know begging and pleading won't get them anywhere.

✔ Negotiate occasionally if your kids want you to bend the rules. For example, if they want you to drive them to a shopping mall when you've announced that the house taxi is parked for the duration, tell them you'll drive if they spend an extra half-hour (the time it takes to drive there and back) folding and putting away laundry. In this way they will learn to respect others' rights and time constraints.

Assume that the following requests violate the limits you have decided upon and deal with them accordingly. Admittedly, real life situations are not resolved so neatly; complicating factors always seem to muddy the waters.

1. Your daughter usually walks to school. On rainy days you drive her, but today she asks you to drive her and it's not raining. You aren't dressed yet and had planned to go to exercise class. What do you say?

2. At six P.M. on Friday night, some friends that you're not close to call and say they would like to bring a six-pack or a bottle of wine and watch a video with you and your husband. Both of you were looking forward to a quiet family night. What do you say?

3. You have a needy and loquacious friend who always calls just as you're preparing dinner. You have never been able to get her off the phone. What do you say?

4. Your son announces at eight P.M. that you are supposed to bake two dozen cookies for class tomorrow. He's sorry he forgot to tell you earlier. You have none of the necessary ingredients. What do you do?

5. Your daughter is graduating from high school and wants to have a big bash for the whole graduating senior class, which means ninety kids. This is about sixty kids too many in your opinion. She's persistent. How do you handle it?

Making Requests

Making a direct request is fundamental to being assertive. How else can people give us what we want if we haven't asked? As logical as that sounds, many of us choose instead to beat around the bush, hint, sulk, or use other ploys in hopes that others will read our minds. We usually end up disappointed. Why? Not because our loved ones are mean or selfish, but because other people are usually so caught up with their own agendas they don't have the time or interest (not to mention the ability!) to read our minds.

Don't beat around the bush as Martha did one Friday when she and her husband received a sailing invitation. She approached her husband, Jim, in this roundabout way: "Jim, sailing on Sunday with the Browns really sounds good. I don't know if I can go though. I suppose we could go, if I just didn't have so many commitments on Saturday—all the ball games and cooking for the track banquet. Well, I suppose we could go, maybe if I start running errands and cooking today and no other disasters occur in the meantime."

What in the world is this babbling supposed to mean? Is it any wonder Jim missed the implied request in all this gobblygook? After several hours of Martha's silent treatment, he found out. What Martha was trying to say—but didn't—

was this: "Jim, would you take charge of all the kids' activities on Saturday so that I can catch up on my errands? Then we can go sailing on Sunday."

Tips for Making Requests

- ✔ Make sure your requests are specific as to time, place and other requirements. Include in your request the good consequences that will follow.

- ✔ When making requests of your children, make sure you provide them with the follow-through help necessary for them to get the job done.

- ✔ Don't jump to the conclusion that the person you're making a request of will be angry with you for asking. He or she can always refuse the request.

- ✔ Try making a request every day. Some ideas: Ask for cooperation from your husband, children, and/or parents. Ask to borrow an item. Ask for a favor. Ask for a little tender, loving care.

- ✔ Once in a while make an outrageous request just to keep the people around you on their toes. Asking your husband to carry out the trash or to clean up the dinner dishes is not an outrageous request; asking him to miss Monday night football to take the Indian Princesses caroling might be; asking him to take them snow camping definitely is! But you never know. One of the great mysteries of life is people's capacity to respond in unexpected ways.

Receiving a Compliment

It is not immodest, unladylike or conceited to acknowledge and show your enjoyment at receiving praise. A simple but elegant "Thank you" covers most compliment occasions. "How kind of you to say so" and "That really makes me feel good" are also good stock responses.

Tips for Accepting Praise

✔ Look the complimenter in the eye when you thank him or her. Try not to gaze off into the distance or stare at the floor.

✔ Acknowledge that you deserve the praise. Try not to say "It was nothing" or "All the credit really goes to my committee" unless you really made no contribution.

✔ Don't feel pressured by a compliment to come right back with a compliment. Avoid obviously false compliments even if your intention is to make someone feel good.

Accepting Criticism

Criticism—whether you're giving or receiving—is never fun. But if we think of criticism as useful information that we can use to enhance our personal growth and the quality of our relationships, criticism can be constructive. As we gain in self-confidence, we can acknowledge our own faults without feeling rejected. Others will then correctly perceive that we are interested people who are open to new ideas and willing to change and grow.

Tips for Accepting Criticism

✔ Learn to separate valid from invalid criticism. First of all, make sure you understand exactly what has been said. Try to understand the other person's point of view and why he or she said it. If the criticism has a familiar ring, perhaps it is valid and you should be doing something about it. Second, consider the source: If your critic is notorious for making ridiculous statements or has other hidden reasons to find fault with you, look for the grain of truth that is present in most criticisms, then forget it. Garbage in. Garbage out.

✔ Don't interpret every comment as criticism. If your husband mentions what a hefty income Bob's wife Judy makes, don't immediately assume he wants you to go back to work.

✔ When responding to valid criticism, acknowledge that the criticism is realistic. Then respond with what you are doing (or intend to do) to work on the problem. If you are criticized for a trait or behavior that bothers others but that you think is an asset, tell the critic why you are not motivated to change.

✔ When responding to invalid criticism or putdowns, you have three basic choices:

1. Ignore the remark or laugh it off. With any luck your attacker will appear petty and mean-spirited.

2. Fire back a witty retort if you're one of the few fast enough on her feet to come up with something appropriate at the moment—not eight hours later in bed. Be careful with responding in kind: You may end up looking petty and mean-spirited yourself.

3. Make a direct, assertive remark such as, "I'm offended by that comment" or "I didn't appreciate your making that comment in front of the group" or "Why would you say such a hurtful thing?!"

✔ Have some stock phrases ready so you won't be caught speechless: "Was that a putdown?" or "Why are you in such a bad mood today?" are generic retorts. Add to your list as you hear good ones.

How would you handle the following criticisms?

1. A significant person in your life forgets your birthday or anniversary—again.

2. Your husband criticizes how you look.

3. Your child tells you you're not as nice as his best friend's mother.

4. An idea you offered at a meeting is shot down.

5. You apply for admission to an organization or a school and are turned down.

6. You have completed a report for a committee you're on but are told you need to do it over because it is inadequate.

7. You have just learned indirectly that your son will not be invited to another child's house because of his bad manners and unruly behavior.

Giving Criticism

Constructive criticism is given in the spirit of helping another person or seeking to improve your relationship with that person; it doesn't blame or shame. If there were a workable formula for criticism, it would include the use of "I"-statements to express your feelings about a person's behavior, a description of the specific behavior that is causing the problem, and a description of how that behavior is affecting you. If appropriate, the addition of a positive statement about the person and some possible alternatives to the behavior can go a long way toward getting the other person to modify the behavior which you find unacceptable.

For example, let's say your husband frequently comes home late without calling first. An assertive way of handling the situation might go something like this: "Joe, I really look forward to eating with you every evening and go to a great deal of trouble to have a nice dinner on the table by 6:30. When you don't call and tell me you're going to be late, not only do I worry that you've been in an accident, but I waste a lot of time that I could use for something else. I make phone calls to try and track you down, I make a dinner you won't eat, and I have trouble concentrating on my job with the kids. I don't have a problem with your staying out late for a business dinner, but I do need a phone call as soon as you know you're going to be late. I'll miss your company but at least I can plan accordingly and won't worry." Notice that no one called Joe irresponsible, inconsiderate, or a jerk.

Tips for Giving Criticism

✔ Use "I"-statements to help you communicate assertively. You can't presume to know what other people are thinking or feeling, but you're certainly the expert on your own point of view and unique perspective. By saying, "I'm really disappointed when you back out of plans at the last minute," rather than, "You're a lousy friend," your friend won't feel as defensive and will be more open to your point of view. By describing how you feel about the person's behavior, you also leave the door open for his or her side of things.

✔ Make sure you communicate your point clearly and directly. One trap that the overly tactful critic can fall into is giving such mild criticism that the person she has just criticized walks away feeling praised.

✔ Don't avoid giving constructive criticism when it is appropriate; otherwise you will encourage the unsatisfactory behavior. Giving criticism is always uncomfortable, but if the session goes well and the conflict is resolved, both of you will feel relieved.

How would you handle the following situations?

1. Your friend has borrowed money and agreed to repay it but has not.

2. You are co-chairing a committee, but your partner isn't holding up her end.

3. You are part of a carpool. One woman in it never seems to be able to drive due to a never-ending series of personal emergencies.

4. You are in a playgroup. Because one little boy kicks and bites your daughter regularly and won't listen to the mother in charge, you don't want him in your home anymore. His mother seems oblivious to his destructive behavior.

5. Your friend has been betraying your confidence. You learn that she has been telling acquaintances the details of a nasty fight you had with your husband.

General Tips for Practicing Assertiveness

✔ Try to visualize yourself acting assertively and experiencing positive results. For example, non-assertive thinking might tell you that if you turn down a volunteer job at the school, people will think you're lazy or that you don't care about the school or the children. Think instead: They will appreciate knowing my answer right now and will respect my realistic assessment of the situation.

✔ Observe and talk to people you consider to be assertive.

✔ Practice, practice, practice! Start small: Knowing what to say and when and how to say it is a complex skill that is not easily mastered. Start with a small behavior such as requesting the return of some borrowed items. Work up to trickier, more complex situations such as dealing with a manipulative friend. If at first one tactic doesn't work, try another and then another until you hit upon the solution.

✔ Practice assertive behavior with a friend who will give you feedback. Or practice by yourself in front of a mirror or with a tape recorder or, better still, with a video recorder. You may be astonished that you're not being as assertive as you had thought.

✔ When dealing with your children, make sure you listen to their points of view and to how they feel. Acknowledge that they too have rights.

✔ Scripting is a good strategy for rehearsing assertive behavior. By rewriting a scene in your life you feel you bungled, you are more likely to be more assertive when it happens again. Rehearse out loud. Scripting can also be used to anticipate a situation in which you know you have a tendency to be non-assertive. Determining how things are likely to go and planning your response will help you be more confident when the scene actually takes place.

✔ If you find it very difficult to behave assertively, try reading assertiveness training books, attending a workshop or class, or getting the help of a counselor.

Our self-respect and self-confidence grow with each successful assertive encounter. As we work on our repertoire of assertive skills and take responsibility for communicating our real thoughts and feelings, we feel more in control of our own lives. As we learn to say "no," make requests, receive praise and criticism, and confront in an assertive manner, we are forced to be conscious of what we think and feel about the world and the people in it. Ironically, in the process of getting others to listen to us, we actually become better at listening to others. This fine-tuning of our communication skills—one definition of assertiveness—makes us more effective wives, mothers, friends, co-workers. Best of all, we raise more assertive and therefore effective children who are in the habit of communicating clearly and honestly and who will be able to set and achieve their goals in life.

Exercises for Helping You Practice Assertiveness

1. Do you feel you have enough time to "do your own thing?"

2. In which situations or with which issues do you find it difficult to be assertive? Check those that are trouble areas for you.

   ☐ your husband
   ☐ money issues
   ☐ your mistakes
   ☐ friends

☐ free time

☐ giving praise

☐ men

☐ time alone

☐ receiving praise

☐ women

☐ housework

☐ giving criticism

☐ your parents

☐ sex

☐ receiving criticism

☐ acquaintances

☐ women's rights

☐ working women

☐ political opinions

☐ your children

☐ your achievements

☐ small groups

☐ large groups

3. Ask yourself what keeps you from being more assertive in the areas you checked.

4. Assess your own behavior patterns using this scale:

1 = Always

2 = Most of the time

3 = Sometimes

4 = Almost Never

How often are you assertive?

How often are you aggressive?

How often are you indirectly aggressive?

How often are you passive?

5. Think of three situations where you wanted to say "no" but said "yes" instead. How do you wish you had responded? Be specific, using full sentences.

6. Anticipate three situations in which you will have difficulty saying "no." Write down what you will say.

7. How much are you willing to do for others? What are you currently doing for others? If these two answers are out of balance, what can you do to bring them into balance?

8. Generate a list of five requests that you would like to make. Write down exactly what you would say in your request.

9. Think of three "outrageous" requests you would like to make. Write those down as assertively as you can.

10. Think of a situation or person about which you feel afraid, uncomfortable, angry, helpless, or worried. Come up with a plan of action in which you behave assertively.

11. How do you typically respond to criticism? Think of some criticisms in your past and rewrite the scene so that you behave assertively next time.

14

What Next?

We all live according to our own stories but sometimes
we forget that we are the authors of those stories.
— Beth White on her work leading
support groups for at-home mothers

According to White, part of the reason at-home mothers have difficulties with long-term goals is because they see
this activity as undermining their mothering priorities. Heed-
ing the oft-heard grandmotherly advice to "Enjoy them—they
grow so fast," moms want to enjoy each day to the fullest in
the here and now. But it is precisely because our children do
grow so fast that we should give some thought to what we will
do once they grow less dependent on us. "This is difficult from
an emotional standpoint," says White. "The trick is to enjoy
both the childraising and the planning for the future without
feeling overwhelmed by either." This "trick" of simulta-
neously enjoying both raising children and planning for a life
separate from children is the subject of this chapter.

Why, you might be asking yourself, does a book about
at-home mothers address itself to work outside the home? It's
a fair question. First of all, the vast majority of at-home mothers

will eventually re-enter the workforce. The need to accumulate money for college costs or retirement and an insecure job market practically guarantee that!

Secondly, in order to re-enter the workforce with relative ease after a long stint at home, we need to start doing our homework well in advance of our projected re-entry time. Cramming won't work. A headstart allows us to avoid the full-scale panic and the frantic scramble for a job, any job—no matter how low-pay or low-status—which can occur if we put off the "What next?" question until the last strains of "Pomp and Circumstance" are fading in a high school auditorium. We've all heard the horror stories of "displaced homemakers." Now is the time to seriously consider what kind of job we could really get—not after the first $2,000-a-month college bill comes rolling in.

And third, mental "moonlighting"—exploring career opportunities outside the realm of childrearing and homemaking—provides a refreshing change of pace and exposure to new ideas that can be as stimulating as black coffee.

While we are busy raising the next generation—certainly the biggest of all big goals—why not raise our heads occasionally to look to the future? Why not take a little time while we have the luxury of a few hours in between carpools to learn what jobs we could perform happily and effectively? Why not start now to develop ourselves in ways that can mean future work that truly fits our life, instead of vice versa?

Cardozo reports in her book *Sequencing* that at-home mothers who have worked previously rank "control over my own time" and "desire to do that which is intrinsically rewarding" as their top two criteria in choosing a post-child career (225). Money came in a surprising third, while prestige, advancement, and power came in closer to the bottom. A job that meets these specifications won't just fall into your lap—unless, that is, you believe in the Job Fairy, or you have an adoring uncle who just happens to be a captain of industry and loves to place relatives within his organization. For most of us, the difference between wanting and getting is a function of the time and energy we invest in preparing ourselves.

You have three broad "What Next?" choices for a second-time career:

1. Should you return to your old career?

2. Would you prefer to switch to a different job in your old field?

3. Are you itching to try something completely new?

If you are one of the lucky minority who knows exactly what you want to do and when and how, don't close this book before considering that, as one pundit put it, "The future isn't what it used to be." Death, divorce, and a rapidly changing work environment may mean your plan crashes and burns due to circumstances completely out of your control. Prepare for the unexpected by defining some other line of work that you could enjoy doing and could do well. Always have a Plan B!

Creating Plan A and Plan B need not be a grim exercise in self-criticism—it may even be fun! The process for finding "What Next?" in this chapter is a game of self-exploration: You explore in a guided way what you love to do; then, you find out what career opportunities are related to these activities that you love doing.

Instead of moving in a linear fashion through the process, we will proceed by phases. A straight shot from Point A to Point B isn't possible when our children our pulling our hearts the other way. Less-structured phases reflect the forward and backward motion, the "two steps forward, one step back" path of progress so typical of the process. Phases are flexible enough to absorb the inevitable setbacks, detours, and dead ends. Phase-by-phase we gradually ebb and flow toward our big goals. We plan on two steps forward, one step back; if we get to keep two forward moves, it's frosting on the cake.

In planning for "What Next?" we will work through five phases:

Phase 1: Raising Children Is Enough for Now

Phase 2: Discovering Yourself

Phase 3: Exploring Options

Phase 4: Goalsetting

Phase 5: Taking Small Action Steps

Phase 1: Raising Children Is Enough for Now

In Phase 1, all your energy is directed at coping with the basics: children, marriage, friends, extended family, the house and garden, shopping, cooking, and finding a little time for yourself. For now, this is plenty.

The length of time a woman stays in this phase depends on a host of variables such as her finances, her former career, her emotional state, interests, and the number and spacing of her children. My very own mother—and she is not alone—still thinks a woman should remain in Phase 1 on a permanent basis!

Phase 2: Discovering Yourself

The basic idea here is to discover the following:

- ✔ What working conditions are important to you?
- ✔ What activities do you love?
- ✔ What skills do you enjoy that could expand into the career realm?

Don't limit yourself to what's available "out there!" Don't think that even though you hate working as a nurse, that's your only choice because that's all you know how to do. If you go after a job you're passionate about, you'll be good at it. If you're not, you won't.

What Working Conditions Are Important to You?

Ask yourself the following questions:

- ✔ With what kind of people do you prefer working?

- ✔ What kind of a schedule would work best for you?

- ✔ Do you work well in short spurts, or do you like to work for long periods?

- ✔ Do you work well under pressure?

- ✔ Do you like change and variety or do you prefer routine?

- ✔ Do you have any health, scheduling, or transportation needs that would limit your choice of a working environment?

- ✔ How much money will you need to earn to meet your future financial goals? Can you afford to volunteer your services for a period of time?

- ✔ In what environment do you see yourself working? In a courtroom or at a tree nursery? At home with occasional trips to the office? On the road?

- ✔ Do you prefer to work for a company that manufactures and sells a product or one that provides a service? Would you be more comfortable in a small or large organization? How about quite small? According to Richard Bolles in *What Color is Your Parachute?* organizations with twenty or less employees supply two-thirds of the new jobs.

- ✔ With what fields of knowledge would you prefer to work (e.g., geology or history)?

✔ From the following list, pick the five that are the most important to you.

Independence	Power
Leadership	Expertise
Self-fulfillment	Duty
Nurturing	Friendship
Family	Health
Security	Pleasure
Wealth	Flexibility
Nature	Environment
Beauty	Compassion
Glamour	Popularity
Honesty	Sensitivity
Justice	

Now rank those five. These are your values. Knowing your own values will help you realize with whom and for whom you will feel comfortable working.

What Activities Do You Love?

Maybe you love mothering and homemaking. On the other hand, you may pine for your previous job. Perhaps you love a sport, a hobby, or a pastime like watching rental videos. Perhaps you're fascinated by southeast Asia after having studied it in a course or because you watched the Mel Gibson movie *Living Dangerously.* What follow are exercises designed to help you discover what you love; that knowledge can lead you to a line of work that capitalizes on what you enjoy the most.

1. Refer to the exercises you completed in chapter 10, "Finding Your Passion." These exercises were intended to help you find fulfilling and productive avocations, pastimes, hobbies, and interests as part of your "time for you." They

can also form natural stepping stones to fulfilling work outside the home. Review specifically the exercises What Do You Love?, Listing Ten Positive Personality Traits, Twenty-Five Things to Do Before You Die for clues to what you love. What was the result of these exercises? What activities did you decide to pursue?

2. **The "Top Twenty" Exercise:** Generate a list of at least twenty things you like to do. Items can range from eating popcorn in a movie theater to curling up with a good book to kayaking up the Amazon. Barbara Sher suggests in her book *Wishcraft* that you follow up your list with these questions:

✔ When was the last time you did this activity?

✔ Are you alone or in a group when you do this activity?

✔ What sort of environment are you in? Fast-paced or slow?

✔ Is this activity job-related?

✔ Are you working with people, things, or information?

   Look for patterns in your answers. Try to become aware of your unique pattern of aptitudes and qualities that might expand into the career realm.

3. Refer to your list of personality traits from exercise 2 in chapter 10 (page 150). From these, select the three which represent your most prominent characteristics. Again, see if these fit into your "unique pattern"

What Skills Do You Enjoy That Could Transfer into the Career Realm?

What marketable skills do you have? Your choice of a career should make use of your strongest skills. Fortunately, your strongest skills are usually the ones you enjoy doing. The following exercises will help you identify these enjoyable, marketable skills.

1. Review the list of skills on the following pages. Place a check next to those you do well and enjoy using on a regular basis. When you check off your marketable skills, flesh them out with an object and add other qualifiers. Just saying you're good at training doesn't say much. Are you good at training ivy to grow in certain ways or at training groups of sales reps? If you can organize, do you organize kitchens and closets or trade shows? If you're interested in learning a skill, note that as well. When you are through, pick what you consider to be your six strongest and enjoyable skills.

Marketable Skills

Type of Skill	What/Comments	Do Well	Enjoy
Communicating			
Advising		_____	_____
Arbitrating		_____	_____
Coaching		_____	_____
Corresponding		_____	_____
Counseling		_____	_____
Demonstrating		_____	_____
Developing rapport		_____	_____
Editing		_____	_____
Empowering		_____	_____
Inspiring		_____	_____
Intervening in crisis		_____	_____
Interviewing		_____	_____
Listening		_____	_____
Managing conflict		_____	_____
Mediating		_____	_____
Mentoring		_____	_____
Negotiating		_____	_____
Networking		_____	_____
Persuading		_____	_____
Presenting ideas		_____	_____
Relating with clients		_____	_____
Relating with community		_____	_____
Relating with customers		_____	_____
Relating with the public		_____	_____
Recording		_____	_____
Recruiting		_____	_____
Referring		_____	_____
Reporting		_____	_____
Speaking		_____	_____
Speaking publicly		_____	_____
Taking instructions		_____	_____
Teaching		_____	_____
Training		_____	_____
Translating		_____	_____
Using diplomacy and tact		_____	_____
Wordprocessing		_____	_____
Writing		_____	_____

Marketable Skills (continued)

Type of Skill	What/Comments	Do Well	Enjoy
Coordinating			
Adapting		_____	_____
Combining		_____	_____
Expanding		_____	_____
Gaining cooperation		_____	_____
Improving		_____	_____
Joining		_____	_____
Scheduling		_____	_____
Serving as liaison		_____	_____
Team-building		_____	_____
Working with Data			
Analyzing finances		_____	_____
Appraising		_____	_____
Assessing		_____	_____
Auditing		_____	_____
Budgeting		_____	_____
Computing		_____	_____
Correcting		_____	_____
Cost accounting		_____	_____
Cost analyzing		_____	_____
Creating financial innovations		_____	_____
Developing control systems		_____	_____
Developing procedures		_____	_____
Developing systems		_____	_____
Diagnosing		_____	_____
Evaluating		_____	_____
Financial planning		_____	_____
Financing		_____	_____
Judging		_____	_____
Managing details		_____	_____
Managing finances		_____	_____
Measuring		_____	_____
Preparing budgets		_____	_____
Recordkeeping		_____	_____
Reviewing finances		_____	_____
Setting standards		_____	_____
Taking inventory		_____	_____

Marketable Skills (continued)

Type of Skill	What/Comments	Do Well	Enjoy
Managing/Directing			
Advising			
Appointing			
Approving			
Assigning			
Conducting			
Decision-making			
Delegating			
Developing staff			
Directing			
Empowering			
Evaluating			
Facilitating groups			
Formulating policy			
Goal setting			
Governing			
Helping			
Human resource planning			
Implementing			
Initiating			
Instructing			
Interpreting policy			
Leading			
Managing			
Motivating			
Presiding			
Project managing			
Serving as an agent of change			
Supervising			
Team-building			
Working well with ambiguity			
Planning			
Analyzing			
Conceptualizing			
Creating			
Designing			
Designing systems			
Developing policy			

Marketable Skills (continued)

Type of Skill	What/Comments	Do Well	Enjoy
Planning (continued)			
Estimating		_____	_____
Initiating		_____	_____
Innovating		_____	_____
Inventing		_____	_____
Researching		_____	_____
Surveying		_____	_____
Organizing			
Administering		_____	_____
Analyzing problems		_____	_____
Arranging		_____	_____
Cataloging		_____	_____
Categorizing		_____	_____
Classifying		_____	_____
Collecting		_____	_____
Developing		_____	_____
Developing projects		_____	_____
Designing improvements		_____	_____
Executing		_____	_____
Setting priorities		_____	_____
Sorting		_____	_____
Troubleshooting		_____	_____
Other Skills			
Assisting		_____	_____
Baking		_____	_____
Caregiving		_____	_____
Cleaning		_____	_____
Consulting		_____	_____
Cooking		_____	_____
Decorating		_____	_____
Developing training techniques		_____	_____
Dramatizing		_____	_____
Drawing		_____	_____
Fundraising		_____	_____
Helping others		_____	_____
Imagining		_____	_____
Investing		_____	_____

Marketable Skills (continued)

Type of Skill	What/Comments	Do Well	Enjoy
Other Skills (continued)			
Managing information		_____	_____
Managing sales		_____	_____
Marketing		_____	_____
Negotiating contracts		_____	_____
Painting		_____	_____
Performing		_____	_____
Playing an instrument		_____	_____
Playing games		_____	_____
Printing		_____	_____
Problem solving		_____	_____
Producing something		_____	_____
Reading		_____	_____
Refinishing		_____	_____
Repairing		_____	_____
Researching and analyzing		_____	_____
Transporting		_____	_____
Traveling		_____	_____
Visualizing		_____	_____
Working with animals		_____	_____
Working with your hands		_____	_____
Other		_____	_____

2. **Significant Event Activity:** Your past experiences can be helpful in identifying the traits and skills that have contributed to your success. Identify two key successes in your personal or professional life. These events should be significant accomplishments for you—not first prize, the presidency of this or that, or the world record. It could be learning to roller skate or ride a bicycle, designing a flower or vegetable garden, or making the decision to move out of your parents' home to an apartment of your own. Describe the situation or problem you had at the time; then describe in detail the steps you took to solve the problem. Then add how everything turned out. Now, for the tricky part: What traits or skills did you use?

3. If you have trouble analyzing the skills you used in achieving what you did in the previous exercise, try the following:

✔ Get together with one or two friends and work through the Significant Event Activity together. Others may be able to assess your positive traits more objectively than you can.

✔ Order the I CAN book series by Ruth B. Ekstrom. The books in this series list homemaking skills according to business roles and titles, information especially helpful for women who have never held outside employment. Write to the Educational Testing Service, Publication Order Services, CN 6736, Princeton, NJ 08541-6736, to order the series, which includes:

HAVE Skills Women's Workbook: Finding Jobs Using Your Homemaking and Volunteer Work Experience

How To Get College Credit for What You Have Learned as a Home-maker and Volunteer

HAVE Skills Employer's Guide: Matching Women and Jobs

HAVE Skills Counselor's Guide: Helping Women Find Jobs Using Their Homemaking and Volunteer Work Experience.

4. If the above exercise doesn't work and you still have no clue about your skills and aptitudes, you may have to pay a professional career counselor or tester to help you. Try the career center or counseling office at a local college for more leads.

Phase 3: Exploring Your Options

Identifying personal interests and skills opens doors by presenting new options. First, look at your existing interests and skills to see if they suggest career options you are already aware of, then expand your options through research. Usually, people are only aware of a small percentage of the jobs available in a particular field. Your job in Phase 3 is to find out about those other jobs. You can then decide if they are realistic options based on the inventory of personal traits and skills that you did in Phase 2.

How do you go about this research? Here are some ideas:

✔ Head for your local library and read up on different job titles, organizations and businesses you're interested in. Ask a friendly research librarian for assistance in finding directories or journals related to your interests.

✔ Talk to friends, acquaintances, people you do business with, anyone you meet about what you're interested in. Are thirty sets of eyes and

ears better than one? Are one hundred even
better? You bet.

✔ Once you've learned everything you can from
reading, consider setting up an informational
interview with someone in the field. Use your
network of contacts to get leads on the names of
people doing what you think you might want
to do. Take this step after you are pretty far
along in the process. Never waste someone's
time with questions you could get from printed
material.

The next step is to eliminate options that don't fit in with
your working condition criteria, which you will establish in
Phase 4, and those that don't mesh with your needs and skills.
Now that you've narrowed the field, pick five options. From
those five, pick the one you would love to do the most, the
second most, etc.

"This Is Your Life" Exercise (courtesy of Beth White)

Write at least three future autobiographies based on the
career options you've selected. The purpose of this exercise is
not to figure out the detailed logistics of your plan—far too
difficult to pin down precisely this early in the game—but to
visualize all that will be going on in your life so that your final
decision will take those into account. Use the following ground
rules:

✔ Don't be super-realistic. Paint with a big brush,
making broad assumptions and taking it on
faith that you'll be doing what you hope you'll
be doing.

✔ Ask yourself what you and each member of
your family will be doing one year from now,
three years from now, five years from now, ten
years from now. With this information you can
time your moves more strategically. For

example, if your kids are fifteen and thirteen now, in five years you may have two kids in college. If you were planning to go for your Master's, perhaps you should do it now, so that you avoid paying tuition for three! If you think you want to go back to your old accounting firm in five years, think about what ages your two and five year olds will be, about what their lives will look like. What will you do with the kids in the summer? On vacation? After school? What other kinds of family situations might you be facing (caring for a sick parent, a job transfer, less out-of-town travel for your husband, more money to hire outside help)?

✔ Don't be discouraged by the stumbling blocks you may discover; the first step in solving a problem is to identify it.

Phase 4: Setting Goals

Setting long-term goals helps us prioritize so that we can make decisions about where to expend time and energy. From the five options you discovered in Phase 3, write down your top two long-term goals. Here are some examples:

✔ to run a wallpapering business from my home

✔ to own and operate a pre-school

✔ to start a line of designer hand-knit sweaters

✔ to work in the office of a plant nursery

✔ to be a sales representative for baby formula

✔ to write software on a contract basis

Write out goal statements for your top two options and say them aloud.

What Next?

Congratulations: You've got Plan A and Plan B!

Now you need to figure out what needs to be done to achieve your goals. Brainstorm for a few minutes, using the following questions to guide you:

- ✔ How can I gain further knowledge about this field?
- ✔ What contacts do I currently have?
- ✔ What habits and practices should I establish in order to make my goal happen?
- ✔ What skills do I need to gain to be effective in this job? How can I get them?
- ✔ Can a volunteer job help me gain these skills?
- ✔ Do I need more education or training?
- ✔ What organizations or groups could I join that are related to this area?
- ✔ What, if anything, do I need to purchase?
- ✔ Is there something I could produce (make a sample of, learn a process for) that would be good training?
- ✔ What sort of reading would be useful?
- ✔ What organizations or businesses in my area offer jobs in my field?

Make a list of all you might need to do to achieve your goal. My goal, for example, was "to publish a support book for at-home mothers." This is what my list looked like:

- ✔ take a writing class
- ✔ go to a writer's workshop
- ✔ publish a magazine article
- ✔ network with other writers
- ✔ join a writer's group

- ✔ subscribe to a writer's journal
- ✔ improve wordprocessing skills
- ✔ buy a computer and software
- ✔ interview at-home mothers
- ✔ research my topic
- ✔ write the book
- ✔ find a publisher

After you make your list, organize the projects into some workable sequence so that you can start scheduling them into your daily life. Important: Do not allow yourself to be overwhelmed by the size of the task ahead of you. Remember that "the goose is plucked feather by feather." Your mantra at this point should be "one foot in front of the other." (Going back to my goal, you are reading this book, aren't you?)

Your Plan A is not set in cement. The best-laid plans may not work out in real life the way they do on paper. Frequently we don't have enough information at the start or we aren't thinking clearly about the more difficult steps. Therefore, we need to concentrate on a detailed plan of action for the first few projects. After we complete those, we can re-evaluate the next several moves.

Phase 5: Taking Small Action Steps

Once you have formulated your goal and decided how to achieve it, break the intermediary steps into small, manageable pieces. Then break those pieces into super-small action items that you can tackle one at a time. What is the "trick" that will allow you to keep your family as your top priority while at the same time accomplishing your goals with a minimum of strain and pain? The steps must be small enough so that you can squeeze them into whatever scraps of time are available. For example, if one of the steps on your list is to take a writing course at a local college, the list of Super-Small Action Items might look like this:

- ✔ call the college to order a schedule of courses
- ✔ select the appropriate course
- ✔ fill out the registration form and send it in
- ✔ write down the days class will meet on your calendar
- ✔ arrange for childcare during classtimes
- ✔ complete the course work

If you need more information about the courses before you can select the appropriate one, put "Call the college English department" down on your list. If even that's too much to fit into your day, at least get the needed telephone numbers ready.

After you break those tasks down into specific, super-small action items, get out your calendar and write down what you're going to do *today!* Discovering your passions, analyzing your aptitudes and mulling over possible goals are fascinating ways to pass the time. But they are worth very little in a practical sense unless you follow them up with action. Commit yourself to following through on the Super- Small Action Items. "One foot in front of the other" will get you where you where you want to go—just get that foot out there!

Tips for Goalplanning (courtesy of Beth White)

- ✔ Always put your goal in writing. Keep written goals where you can refer to them easily in your daily planning.

- ✔ When you set a goal, always set a deadline. "By when will I commit to have this done?" Set your target date.

- ✔ If you miss your deadline, *reschedule.* Set a new deadline right away. There is no limit to the number of times you're allowed to reschedule. (If you're really stuck, just set a deadline for when you'll set the new deadline.)

✔ Set both short-term (one-year) and long-term (five-year) goals. When you set goals for five years or longer, look at how old your children will be by then. How old will you be? How old will your parents be? How will all of this impact your life?

✔ Set at least one ambitious goal. Really stretch. Sometimes at-home mothers often keep their commitments and goals too small, too short-term. It doesn't matter that you volunteer (rather than be paid) if you're really getting an opportunity to build skills. Think of taking on a big project—for pay or not—as adding to your resume.

✔ Build a network of support. Let others know what you're thinking about. By including others in your exploration, you dramatically increase the ideas, opportunities and contacts available to you and become more "accountable" for your progress.

✔ Go to a workshop or conference. Opportunities abound for an intensive experience in a field you might wish to explore. While you're at it, look around at who else is in this field. Is this a group you would find stimulating?

✔ Develop and practice a short (1- to 1½-minute) speech or introduction in which you explain to others what you're interested in doing. For example, "I'm exploring options in the writing field." Tell what you're currently doing and what questions you have; then end by asking for your listeners' thoughts and opinions. Many at-home mothers feel they mustn't include themselves in any conversation about careers when, in fact, we're doing what most working people do every three to five years—planning a career change.

I would like to end this chapter with a send-off by our old buddy, the late, great Dr. Seuss. In his bestselling guidebook to life, *Oh, The Places You'll Go!* the good doctor dispenses some advice useful for children of all ages as they set out in new directions. He warns us not to put off getting going or we might end up stuck in the Waiting Place, loaded with people "waiting for the fish to bite / or waiting for wind to fly a kite / or waiting around for Friday night...." As you forge ahead with your plans to explore new horizons, these words might form a suitable motto: "You have brains in your head. / You have feet in your shoes. / You can steer yourself / any direction you choose." And will you succeed? "Yes! You will, indeed! / (98 and ¾ percent guaranteed.)"

Recommended Reading

Arden, Lynie. *The Work-at-Home Sourcebook*. Boulder, Colorado: Live Oak Publications, 1990.

Bolles, Richard. *What Color Is Your Parachute?* Berkeley, CA: Ten Speed Press, 1991.

Behr, Marion, and Wendy Lazar. *Women Working Home: The Homebased Business Guide and Directory*. Edison, New Jersey: Women Working Home, Inc., 1983.

Brabec, Barbara. *Homemade Money: The Definitive Guide to Success in a Home Business*. White Hall, Virginia: Betterway Publications, Inc., 1984.

Mattson, Ralph, and Arthur Miller. *Finding a Job You Can Love*. Nashville, Tennessee: Thomas Nelson Publishers, 1982.

Schepp, Brad. *The Telecommuter's Handbook*. New York: Pharos Books, 1990.

15

Making It Work for You

There's no place like home.
>— Dorothy in *The Wizard of Oz*

A*t-Home Motherhood: Making It Work for You* confirms, I hope, that your choice to stay home can be the right move for you. At-home motherhood can work for your family. What could be more right than giving your children the best possible start in life by offering them your continual presence, guidance, and support in their early years? What could be better than creating a treasure of shared memories with your children? More wonderful than rediscovering the joy and excitement and mystery of the world we live in through the eyes of your children?

You can also make at-home mother work for you as an individual, if you keep moving and growing. I believe that *movement*—physical, emotional, intellectual, spiritual—is as essential as oxygen for our well-being as women. If we are to truly *live* our lives, we must use home base as the start-off for movement—both within and without. Modern society tells us that to go home is to go stale. Wrong. Home is where we have the freedom to spend our time doing what we are passionate about. Society also tells us that to leave the high-pressure world of the full-time employed is to grow rusty. Wrong again. Home is where we can nurture new talents and develop new skills that can be applied when we return to our former careers, if we choose.

At-home motherhood presents extraordinary opportunities to grow: We expand and deepen our commitments in our roles as mothers, wives, friends and members of the community; we learn the practical skills to apply to the "business" aspects of homemaking: maintaining the home, shopping, cooking, and financial planning. While we adapt to the changing needs of our families, we ourselves mature as individuals in our own right. Exploring fresh possibilities for expressing and developing ourselves, we keep our minds, hearts, spirits and bodies strong. Unstructured time at home enables us to delve more deeply and productively into our various roles. We're right in the thick of life. And we're on the move.

How will you know it's working for you, that you're moving in the right direction? When you're so caught up in the tumble of daily life that you catch yourself forgetting for long stretches of time the "previous life" that you once might have longed for; when you feel sad for women who are missing out on most of their child's waking day; when you have your fingers in so many pies with so many people that you haven't dusted for weeks and can't see when you're going to have time; when your latest project is enough of a stretch that, when you wake up in the morning, you're a little bit scared—then you know it's working for you. It doesn't get any better than this!

Resources

At-Home Motherhood

Cahill, Mary Ann. *The Heart Has Its Own Reasons*. Franklin Park, Illinois: La Leche League International, 1983.

Cardozo, Arlene Rossen. *Sequencing*. New York: Macmillan Publishing, 1986.

Davidson, Christine. *Staying Home Instead*. Lexington, Massachussets: Lexington Books, D. C. Heath and Co., 1986.

Parenting

Baldwin, Rahima. *You Are Your Child's First Teacher*. Berkeley, California: Celestial Arts, 1988.

Brazelton, T. Barry. *Toddlers and Parents*. New York: Delacourt Press, 1974.

Dobson, Fitzhugh. *How to Parent*. Los Angeles: Nash Publishing Co., 1971.

Elkind, David. *The Hurried Child: Growing Up Too Fast Too Soon*. Redding, Massachussets: Addison-Wesley, 1981.

Jones, Molly M. *Guiding Your Child from Two to Five*. New York: Harcourt Brace, 1967.

Leach, Penelope. *Your Baby and Child from Birth to Age Five*. New York: Alfred A. Knopf, 1978.

White, Burton. *The First Three Years of Life*. New York: Prentice-Hall Press, 1985.

Women's Issues

DeBeauvoir, Simone. *The Second Sex*. Translated by H. M. Parshley. New York: Bantam, 1968.

French, Marilyn. *The Women's Room*. London: Andre Deutsch, 1978.

Friedan, Betty. *The Feminine Mystique*. New York: Norton, 1963.

————. *The Second Stage*. New York: Summit Books, 1981.

Gilligan, Carol. *In a Different Voice*. Cambridge, Massachussets: Harvard University Press, 1982.

Hochschild, Arlie. *The Second Shift*. New York: Viking-Penguin, Inc., 1989.

Hunt, Morton. *Her Infinite Variety*. New York and Evanston: Harper & Row, 1962.

Kleiman, Carol. *Women's Networks*. New York: Lippincott and Crowell, Publishers, 1980.

Leghorn, Lisa, and Katherine Parker. *Woman's Worth*. Boston: Routledge and Kegan, 1981.

Pogrebin, Letty Cottin. *Family Politics: Love and Power on Intimate Frontiers*. New York: McGraw-Hill, 1983.

Steinem, Gloria. *Outrageous Acts and Everyday Rebellions*. New York: Holt, Rinehart and Winston, 1983.

Theroux, Phyllis. *Peripheral Visions*. New York: Morrow, 1982.

Psychology/Self-Help

Austin, Nancy, and Stanlee Phelps. *The Assertive Woman*. San Luis Obispo, California: Impact Publishers, 1987.

Bauer, Jean. *How to Be an Assertive (Not Aggressive) Woman in Life, in Love, and on the Job*. New York: Rawson Associates Publishers, Inc., 1976.

Bender, Sue. *Plain and Simple*. San Francisco: Harper & Row, 1989.

Burns, David. *Intimate Connections*. New York: William Morrow & Co., Inc., 1985.

Dix, Carol. *The New Mother Syndrome*. New York: Doubleday & Co., 1985.

Dowling, Colette. *Cinderella Complex* New York: Summit Books, 1981.

————. *Perfect Women*. New York: Summit Books, 1988.

Gellman, Meryle, and Diane Gage. *The Confidence Quotient*. New York: World Almanac Publications, 1985.

L'Engle, Madeleine. *A Circle of Quiet*. New York: Ferrar, Straus, Giroux, 1972.

Lindbergh, Anne Morrow. *Gifts from the Sea*. New York: Pantheon Books, 1975.

Norwood, Robin. *Women Who Love Too Much*. Los Angeles: Jeremy P. Tarcher, Inc., 1985.

Shaevitz, Marjorie Hausen. *The Superwoman Syndrome*. New York: Warner Books, 1989.

Sheehy, Gail. *Passages*. New York: E. P. Dutton & Co., Inc., 1974.

Swigart, Jane. *The Myth of the Good Mother*. New York: Doubleday, 1991.

Home Management

Barnes, Emilie. *Survival for Busy Women*. Eugene, Oregon: Harvest House Publishers, 1986.

Bittinger, Marvin L., and William B. Rudolph. *Consumer Smarts*. Woodbury, New York: Barron's Education Series, 1979.

Culp, Stephanie. *How to Get Organized When You Don't Have the Time*. Cincinnati: F & W Publications, 1986.

Gorman, Charlotte. *The Frugal Mind*. Denton, Texas: Nottingham Books, 1990.

Klein, David and Marymae. *Supershopper*. New York: Praeger Publishers, 1971.

Porter, Sylvia. *Sylvia Porter's Money Book*. Garden City, New York: Doubleday & Co., 1975.

Schwannhauser, Mark. "Day Care Woes Hit Parents." *San Jose Mercury News* (February 14, 1993): E1.

Fitness

Cooper, Kenneth. *The Aerobics Program for Total Well-Being*. New York: M. Evans & Co, 1982.

Glover, Bob, and Jack Shepherd. *The Family Fitness Handbook*. New York: Penguin Books, 1989.

Goalsetting/Career Planning

Arden, Lynie. *The Work-at-Home Sourcebook*. Boulder, Colorado: Live Oak Publications, 1990.

Behr, Marion, and Wendy Lazar. *Women Working Home: The Homebased Business Guide and Directory*. Edison, New Jersey: Women Working Home, Inc., 1983.

Bolles, Richard. *What Color Is Your Parachute?* Berkeley, California: Ten Speed Press, updated annually.

Brabec, Barbara. *Homemade Money: The Definitive Guide to Success in a Home Business*. White Hall, Virgnia: Betterway Publications, Inc., 1984.

Mattson, Ralph, and Arthur Miller. *Finding a Job You Can Love*. Nashville: Thomas Nelson Publishers, 1982.

Schepp, Brad. *The Telecommuter's Handbook*. New York: Pharos Books, 1990.

Sher, Barbara. *Wishcraft*. New York: Ballantine Books, 1979.

Index